HOTSPOTS
KENYA

Indian Ocean Resorts

Written by David Watson. Original photography by David Watson

Published by Thomas Cook Publishing
A division of Thomas Cook Tour Operations Limited
Company registration no. 1450464 England
The Thomas Cook Business Park, Unit 9, Coningsby Road,
Peterborough PE3 8SB, United Kingdom
Email: books@thomascook.com, Tel: + 44 (0) 1733 416477
www.thomascookpublishing.com

Produced by Cambridge Publishing Management Limited
Burr Elm Court, Main Street, Caldecote CB23 7NU

ISBN: 978-1-84157-977-1

First edition © 2008 Thomas Cook Publishing
Text © Thomas Cook Publishing
Maps © Thomas Cook Publishing/PCGraphics (UK) Limited

Project Editor: Karen Fitzpatrick
Production/DTP: Steven Collins

Printed and bound in Spain by GraphyCems

Cover photography © moodboard/Corbis

CONTENTS

INTRODUCTION 5
Getting to know Kenya: Indian
    Ocean resorts................................8
The best of Kenya:
    Indian Ocean resorts 10
Symbols key 12

RESORTS 13
Lamu 15
Malindi 25
Watamu 37
Kilifi 45
Mombasa North Coast................49
Diani & Tiwi Beaches 57
Wasini Island & Shimoni............64

EXCURSIONS 67
Land & marine safaris 69
Masai Mara National Reserve 71
Nairobi & Lewa...............................76
Amboseli National Park..............84
Tsavo East and West National
    Parks..89
Shimba Hills National
    Reserve...93

LIFESTYLE...................................95
Food & drink 96
Menu decoder 98
Shopping...101
Children 105
Sports & activities.......................107
Festivals & events.......................109

PRACTICAL INFORMATION 111
Accommodation.............................112
Preparing to go..............................114
During your stay 118

INDEX..125

MAPS
Kenya 6
Lamu Town.......................................14
Malindi...26
Watamu...36
Mombasa North Coast 48
Diani & Tiwi Beaches...................56
Excursions 68

WHAT'S IN YOUR GUIDEBOOK?

Independent authors Impartial, up-to-date information from our travel experts who meticulously source local knowledge.

Experience Thomas Cook's 165 years in the travel industry and guidebook publishing enriches every word with expertise you can trust.

Travel know-how Contributions by thousands of staff around the globe, each one living and breathing travel.

Editors Travel-publishing professionals, pulling everything together to craft a perfect blend of words, pictures, maps and design.

You, the traveller We deliver a practical, no-nonsense approach to information, geared to how you really use it.

THE AUTHOR

David Watson first visited the coast of Kenya in the 1960s as a postgraduate student and since then has lived in all of the East African countries. In addition to Thomas Cook publications, David is mapmaker, photographer and writer for Jacana Maps safari guides.

 Beached boats at Shela

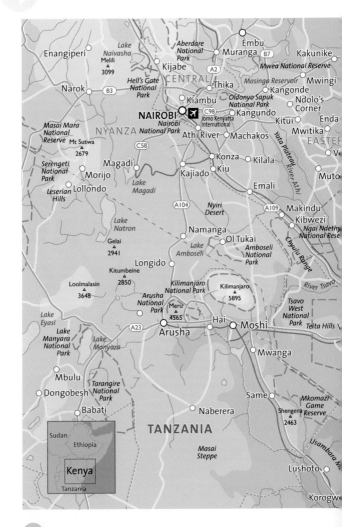

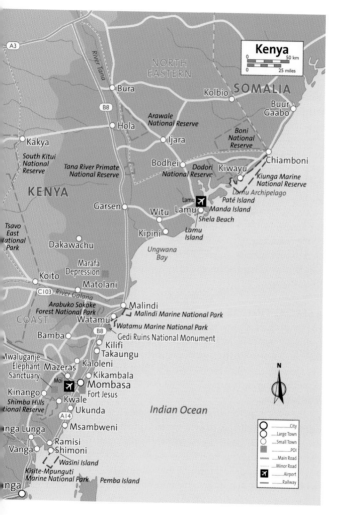

Getting to know Kenya: Indian Ocean resorts

The area of Kenya bordering the Indian Ocean and known as Kenya Coast lies just a few degrees south of the equator, and so enjoys high temperatures all year round, with sunshine guaranteed during most months. The warm currents of the Indian Ocean wash the coastline; an almost continuous coral-sand beach runs down its entire 400-km (250-mile) length, and a coral reef fringes it, broken only where rivers enter the sea. For diving, snorkelling and deep-sea fishing, this is one of the great locations of the world. Next to the beaches lie shallow lagoons, flooded afresh every high tide; further out is the reef, beyond which the sea bed plunges into the depths of the ocean.

On the landward side is a narrow coastal plain. North of Mombasa is the Arabuko-Sokoke Forest, one of the only remaining indigenous forests on the coast, and to the south are the wooded Shimba Hills, home to the Shimba Hills National Reserve. Beyond are the high plains of East Africa, with their amazing wildlife: all can be visited as part of a holiday on Kenya's coast.

A SPECIAL CULTURE

The Kenya Coast is home to Swahili culture, where Arabia meets Africa, with other traditions such as those of India and Southeast Asia also in the mix. One result is the Swahili language, which is a blend of Arabic and some African. Most people here also speak English, as well as their local tribal languages such as Giriama, one of the languages of the coastal people.

The religion and much of the coastal culture is Islamic; many women are clothed from head to toe, though others dress in colourful *kikoys* or wraps. Mosques are everywhere, though often it is difficult to distinguish the mosque from the vernacular architecture. In Mombasa and Malindi there are 'old towns', a maze of passages, alleyways and shady courtyards. And at Lamu there are no roads or cars, just a network of donkey-wide lanes for you to explore.

In many places the traditional sailing vessel, the dhow, in its numerous forms, is still the major means of transport: at Lamu and Mombasa especially, it may well become part of your holiday in the form of the dhow trips that offer diving, dolphin-watching or fine dining. The powerful connection with the sea is also evident in the food here. Alongside the abundant supplies of local tropical fruit, the menu consists mainly of fish and shellfish dishes, with lavish use of oriental spices. Those who go fishing can generally enjoy their own catch, cooked in the hotel kitchens.

⬥ *Setting sail: a traditional dhow*

THE BEST OF KENYA: INDIAN OCEAN RESORTS

Kenya's coast has three magical ingredients. It enjoys one of the world's best and longest tropical beaches, with continuous palm-fringed coral sands from Somalia to Tanzania; it is home to the unique Swahili culture, a mix between Africa and the Gulf; and, to top off its charms, most visitors combine 'beach' with 'bush', adding a thrilling African safari to their holiday on the coast.

TOP 10 ATTRACTIONS

- **Dive on some of the world's best reefs** at Kisite-Mpunguti (see page 65).

- **Snorkel over the reef** at Malindi-Watamu Marine National Park (see page 29).

- **Dine on a Tamarind dhow** as you sail around Mombasa Island (see page 54).

- **Follow in Hemingway's footsteps** and fish for blue marlin off Watamu (see page 40).

- **Visit the World Heritage Site of Lamu** and explore its traffic-free lanes and alleyways (see page 15).

- **Experience the eeriness** of mysteriously deserted Gedi old town (see page 38).

- **Hop in a hot-air balloon** to drift noiselessly above the Masai Mara migration herds (see page 71).

- **Lunch on crab claws and lobster** at Wasini Island (see page 66).

- **Come face to face with a black rhino** at Lewa Wildlife Conservation Area (see page 83).

- **Enjoy a romantic dinner on the beach**, under the stars, at almost any resort along the coast.

◆ *Traditional dugouts at Shimoni*

SYMBOLS KEY
The following symbols are used throughout this book:

ⓐ address ☏ telephone 🖷 fax ⓦ website address ⓔ email
🕐 opening times ❶ important

The following symbols are used on the maps:

🄸 information office		⭕ city
✉ post office		⭕ large town
🛍 shopping		○ small town
🛫 airport		■ POI (point of interest)
✚ hospital		— main road
🛇 police station		— minor road
🚌 bus station		— railway
❶ numbers denote featured cafés, restaurants & evening venues			

RESTAURANT CATEGORIES
The symbol after the name of each restaurant listed in this guide
indicates the price of a typical three-course meal without drinks
for one person:
£ up to KSh1,500   ££ KSh1,500–KSh3,000   £££ over KSh3,000

▶ *Coral island at low tide*

RESORTS
Indian Ocean resorts

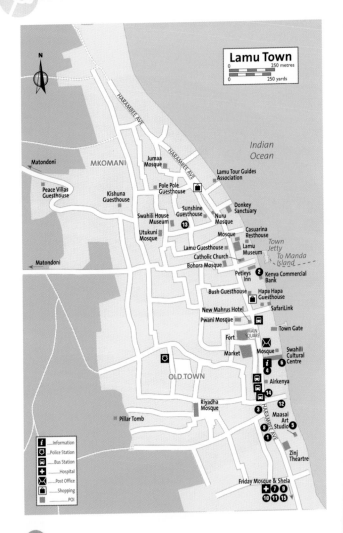

Lamu

Lamu is a small group of islands, almost certainly like nowhere else you have ever been. There are no roads, and to get around you must use a dhow, a donkey – or walk. More recently speed boats have been introduced to the islands, but essentially Lamu is the ideal place to come to unwind, relax and to slow down.

The whole place is dominated by boats and by the sea. Hotels and guesthouses open onto the beach. If you want to travel between Shela and Lamu, your 'taxi' will be a boat; at Shela you will probably have to take off your shoes to paddle ashore. You can sightsee from a dhow, or go diving, snorkelling and fishing.

The UNESCO World Heritage Site of Lamu is one of the world's special places. At least 2,000 years old, the town is a time warp in today's world. There are no roads, and therefore no cars. Streets are a maze of narrow, donkey-wide alleyways. Scattered between the distinctive Swahili courtyard-style houses are over 20 mosques, and a busy commercial scene of cafés and stalls.

The Lamu Cultural Festival is held each November, and at 'Maulidi', the celebration of Mohammed's birthday, the Riyadha Mosque becomes a focus of pilgrimage for Muslims from around the area. The mosque was built at the end of the 19th century by the descendants of Yemeni prophet Habib Swaleh who migrated to Lamu and who introduced a new, freer form of Islamic worship.

BEACHES

Just south of Shela is one of Kenya's best beaches. Most of the waterfront, both at Lamu and at Shela, is taken up by hundreds of dhows and other boats. However, just round the corner from the island's best hotel, Peponi, is the start of 8 km (5 miles) of the most idyllic and largely deserted beach. On the landward side from the sea is a group of huge sand dunes, and the beach itself is a wide strip of coral sand, which you will probably not be sharing with anyone else. Unlike at Malindi or

Mombasa, there are no camel rides, and very few hawkers pestering you to buy tourist trinkets. So if it's peace, quiet, sunshine and sand you are after, Shela Beach is for you.

Hotels such as Peponi and Kijani House also have their own swimming pools, but in general they do not have as much usable beach as you find on the coast further south.

THINGS TO SEE & DO

Fishing
It is possible to arrange fishing trips for a half or full day, and it is best to do this through your hotel.

Historic settlements
There are a number of historic settlements that are of interest to visit, all reachable from Lamu Town. Matondoni is a small, traditional dhow-building village. The round trip takes three hours by motor dhow, five to six hours under sail. Also worth a look are Paté Town, notable for its

---

A SWAHILI EXPERIENCE

If you truly want to enjoy a local experience, an excellent option is to stay in one of the guesthouses that reflect the traditional 'Swahili' model. One of these is Kijani House located on the waterfront at Shela.

Kijani House nestles around a cool and private courtyard, and is based on several traditional houses that have been converted into 11 spacious rooms and suites. Local materials, designs and work methods have been used in the conversion. Set in the courtyard, amongst palms and bougainvilleas, are two discreet swimming pools, making this a delightful and charming retreat.

Both Lamu and Shela have a number of these houses, which make a lovely alternative to mainstream hotels.

Nahabani deserted town ruins, Farza, for its traditional woodwork and Siu for its historical buildings, dating from the 17th to the 19th centuries. Kiwayu, a desert island paradise, can be visited in a day, but is better considered as a get-away-from-it-all excursion over several days (see below).

Kiwayu

Within striking distance of a one-day fast boat trip from Lamu, Kiwayu is the classical desert island, tailor-made for those who want somewhere remote and exclusive. If you have four or five days to spare, you can organise a round trip from Lamu by dhow, much the most romatic option, or you can fly in by Air Kenya or SafariLink from Nairobi, as part of your overall safari plan.

If you want it mostly to yourself, this is the place, with very few other visitors to disturb your tranquillity. Kiunga, north of Kiwayu, is the most northerly and most isolated of the marine national parks and has a host of attractions. There are some amazing coral gardens, with great snorkelling at Kiwayu bay reef, five different species of turtles, a colony of dugongs, and, for bird-lovers, one of the world's main colonies of roseate terns. There are lovely beaches, especially at Ndau Island, just south of Kiwayu.

A day trip to Kiwayu from Lamu is best arranged through your hotel – they will use their normal boatmen. If you are planning a longer trip, involving a stay on the island, this is best arranged through one of the lodges.

Munira Island Camp 🕓 020 512213 🕞 020 512543
Kiwayu Village 🕓 020 600107 🕞 020 606990 🕎 www.kiwayu.com

Lamu Fort

Lamu Fort dates from 1809 when the town was governed by the Sultan of Paté (an island in the Lamu Archipelago), and today it houses a museum, a library and a café specialising in Swahili cuisine. After taking a turn around the fort, head for the adjacent main square, which is the most vibrant open space in Lamu. The terrace at the gate to the fort is the ideal place to take in the busy atmosphere.

ⓐ Main Square, Harambee Avenue ⓛ 08.00–18.00 daily ❶ Small admission charge

Lamu mosques

There are 23 mosques in Lamu Town and six or seven in Shela. Though many are very simple spaces for worship, a few are more elaborate and worth visiting. Most fascinating in its extravagant architecture is the Riyadha Mosque to the north of the town. This is Lamu's newest mosque, dating only from the end of the 19th century, when it was built to commemorate the prophet Habib Swaleh, who migrated to Lamu from Yemen. During the last century it has become a place of regional pilgrimage at the celebration of Mohammed's birthday, Maulidi. The oldest is the Pwani Mosque, built in the 14th century and located near the fort. Most unusual, and located behind Peponi Hotel in Shela, is the rocket-shaped Friday Mosque.

⬥ *The intricate architecture of the Riyadha Mosque*

Lamu Museum

Located just opposite the main jetty, this is reckoned to be the second best museum in Kenya, after the National Museum in Nairobi. It gives a really good insight into Swahili history and culture, especially the history of the dhow. Prize exhibits also include two ceremonial horns, thought to be the oldest surviving musical instruments in black Africa.

ⓐ Lamu waterfront ● 08.00–18.00 daily ❶ Small admission charge

Lamu Town

Time spent exploring the maze of 'streets' of the old town of Lamu is an absolute must during your holiday. You can get a map from the museum as you arrive. Even the main street, Harambee Avenue, is still only wide enough for a donkey. In a couple of hours of gentle meandering and strolling, you will find an utterly fascinating mosaic of houses, cafés, markets and mosques.

Manda Island

Takwa is located on Manda Island, and is approachable by dhow or motorboat at high tide only, sailing through the mangrove channels. It is one of the numerous and apparently thriving settlements on the Kenya Coast that were mysteriously abandoned about 300 years ago. Much of the attraction of these deserted towns lies in the still-unanswered question over exactly why their wealthy and industrious inhabitants left (see page 38).

Among the ruins one can see the Great Mosque, and just outside the wall a pillar tomb which is still visited by pilgrims from nearby Shela, who believe their ancestors came from Takwa.

● 08.00–18.00 daily ❶ Small admission charge

Sunset dhow trips

Dhow trips are especially nice in the late afternoon to early evening, avoiding the heat of the day. One leaves from Lamu or Shela, totally under sail, usually into the Takwa Creek on Manda Island, following the edge of the mangroves. The highlight is normally the lovely (and reliable) sunset off Shela Beach as the sun drops behind the dunes.

● *The ancient alleyways of Shela village*

Swahili House Museum

The Swahili House in Mkomani is a tiny, unpretentious museum that gives a fascinating glimpse into how a Lamu house would have been in the 18th century. In many ways, over the 200 years, not a lot has changed.

ⓐ Mkomani ● 08.00–18.00 daily ❶ Small admission charge

Watersports
Snorkelling
Lots of operators will organise a trip, which is best done through your hotel. There are numerous excellent sites, mainly rocks and reefs, up to a few hours' boat-ride away, ranging from Kinyika Rock, Pazarli to Tinewe Island and Mandatoto.

Other watersports
Other watersports abound, and it is possible to arrange canoeing, waterskiing and windsurfing, all through your hotel.

TAKING A BREAK

In general most visitors to Lamu will eat and drink in their hotel, especially in the evening. Be aware that alcohol will not be available as readily as it is in Western destinations. Also, with boats being the main form of transport in this area, most visits to cafés and coffee shops will be during the day. It is advisable to take a taxi if you do go out in the evening.

DHOWS
The dhow, with its distinctive lateen sail, is the traditional boat of Arabia and the Gulf, and on the East African coast it is as iconic as the coconut palm. Today the sailing dhow is still used by fishermen, and is the commonest means of transport on islands such as Wasini and Lamu. Until the 1960s, large dhows were still used commercially between the Gulf and East Africa, sailing south in the winter and returning north in the summer.

Dhows vary in size from simple dugouts to large vessels with a crew of 30 or more. Ironically, in the high-tech world of the Gulf, the building of traditional wooden dhows is thriving. In Kenya, Lamu is still the major dhow-building and dhow-using port. The sailing dhow remains the workhorse of the Lamu Archipelago.

🔺 *A dhow sail catching the last rays of the sun*

Cafés & restaurants

Coconut Juice Gardens £ ❶ Serves mainly cold drinks, especially ones based on local fruits. Snack food is also available. ⓐ Harambee Avenue ❗ Cash only

Mangrove Café £ ❷ Juices and snacks are the main offerings here. ⓐ Waterfront, near town jetty ❗ Cash only

New Minaa Rooftop Café £ ❸ Another café mainly serving local Swahili food. ⓐ Off Harambee Avenue ❗ Cash only

New Star Restaurant £ ❹ Rather run-down, but the cheapest place to eat in town and a good location for meeting up with locals. ⓐ Harambee Avenue ❗ Cash only

Olympic £ ❺ Popular beachfront café for juices, shakes and snacks. ⓐ Waterfront ❗ Cash only

Seafront Café £ ❻ The place to try a range of cheap local dishes. ⓐ Waterfront, near post office ❗ Cash only

Stopover £ ❼ Lovely seafront, dhow-strewn location. Ultra-friendly service. Simple, but tasty Swahili dishes, seafood a speciality. ⓐ Shela beach, near Kijani House ❗ Cash only

Zam Zam Hotel £ ❽ Local, simple food. It has a few tourists resident, but is generally a great place to make contact with the real inhabitants of Lamu. ⓐ Harambee Avenue ❗ Cash only

Bahari Guesthouse ££ ❾ Located right on the beach. Excellent local food. ⓐ Shela beach, near Peponi Hotel ☎ 042 632046 ❗ Cash only

Island Hotel ££ ❿ Rooftop restaurant. There is no alcohol to be had here, but it does serve appetising Swahili food, especially curries, fish

dishes and vegetarian. The restaurant is candlelit at night.
🅐 Shela beachfront 🕿 042 623290 ❶ Cash only

Kijani House ££ ⓫ Simple fresh food in traditional Swahili house
location overlooking shaded courtyard pool. It also has spacious en-suite
bedrooms and suites (see box page 16). 🕿 042 633235
🌐 www.kijani-house.com ✉ Kijani@africaonline.co.ke
❶ Accepts credit cards

Lamu Palace Restaurant ££ ⓬ Located in the main Lamu hotel,
situated on the central beachfront. Good range of food, from
'as-much-as-you-can-eat' seafood buffets to steaks and Italian dishes.
🅐 Waterfront, near main jetty 🕿 042 633272 ❶ Accepts credit cards

Stone House Rooftop Restaurant ££ ⓭ Part of Stone House Hotel.
Serves especially nice upmarket seafood. 🅐 Mkomani between Donkey
Sanctuary and Swahili House Museum 🕿 042 633544
❶ Accepts credit cards

Whispers At Baraka ££ ⓮ Best coffee in town. Nice cakes and a good
place for breakfast. 🅐 Harambee Avenue 🕿 0121 33355
❶ Accepts credit cards

Peponi House Hotel £££ ⓯ Beautiful location overlooking the entrance
to the Shela-Lamu harbour. Serves alcohol, so a good and popular place
for a cold beer. Excellent food. 🅐 Shela Village, Lamu 0500 🕿 042 633421
🌐 www.peponi-lamu.com ✉ peponi@peponi-lamu.com ❶ Accepts
credit cards

Malindi

Malindi is an historic Swahili town which, from the 12th century onwards, rivalled Mombasa and Paté for the control of the East African coast. The Chinese traded here in the 14th and 15th centuries, and as Malindi was one of the few places to welcome Portuguese explorer Vasco da Gama in 1498, it became the ideal base from which he continued his journey across the Indian Ocean.

In addition to the expected Swahili-Arabic influences in architecture, culture and food, Malindi also has a large Italian population; you are as likely to see pasta and pizza featured on menus as curried prawns.

BEACHES

The best beaches at Malindi are to the south of the town, with easiest public access at Silversands. In addition, many hotels, such as Driftwood, allow non-resident use of their pools, plus beach access for a small fee.

▲ *Vasco da Gama Point*

RESORTS

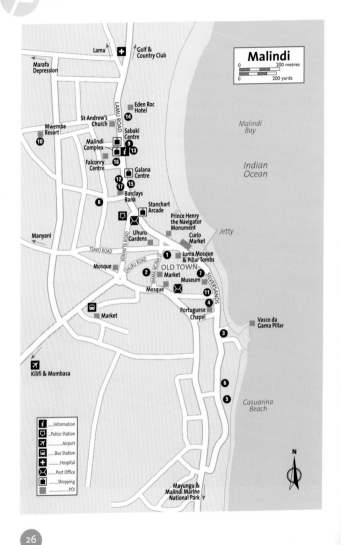

Malindi

0 —————— 200 metres
0 —————— 200 yards

Lamu
Golf & Country Club
Marafa Depression
Eden Roc Hotel
St Andrew's Church
Mwembe Resort
Sabaki Centre
Malindi Complex
Falconry Centre
Galana Centre
Barclays Bank
Stanchart Arcade
Prince Henry the Navigator Monument
Uhuru Gardens
Curio Market
Manyani
Jetty
TSAVO ROAD
Juma Mosque & Pillar Tombs
Mosque
Market
OLD TOWN
Museum
KENYATTA ROAD
UHURU ROAD
MAMA NGINA ST
Mosque
Market
Portuguese Chapel
Vasco da Gama Pillar
Kilifi & Mombasa
Casuarina Beach
SILVERSANDS
Malindi Bay
Indian Ocean
Mayungu & Malindi Marine National Park

N

Key
- *i* ......Information
- ......Police Station
- ✈ ......Airport
- 🚌 ......Bus Station
- ✚ ......Hospital
- ✉ ......Post Office
- 🛍 ......Shopping
- ■ ......POI

THINGS TO SEE & DO

Big-game fishing

Malindi claims to have the best big-game fishing in the world, and the sea fishing club occupies a prominent position on the waterfront. This is the place to go after you catch your record blue marlin or sailfish. Check out the fishing options with your hotel. On the Kenya Coast there is now a voluntary 'tag and release' policy, which is designed to conserve fish stocks (see feature box page 40).

Biking

The land around Malindi is flat, and there are numerous small companies that rent out bikes to holidaymakers. This is a nice way to check out the town and surrounding areas, but watch out for the truly horrendous driving, especially of matatus, the regular Kenyan minibuses. Make arrangements through your hotel.

Curio Market

Located at the northern end of the beach, near the Old Town, this market brings together a group of curio sellers. There's a wide range of goods on offer, but do not buy shells (see page 103).

Diving

Malindi has three PADI-registered dive centres, all located at hotels (Driftwood, Tropical African Dream and Kilili Baharini), which cater for all levels of ability. The best dive times are May to October when the water is beautifully clear. The best dive sites are at Fargialla, Barracuda Point and Shark Point. Diving trips are dependent on the tides, but can be arranged for a whole or half day.

Malindi Old Town

Inland from the northern end of the beach is Malindi Old Town. A warren of alleyways, small coral-rag houses and mosques, it is not as neat and tidy as Lamu, but is still well worth a visit if Swahili culture is new to you.

A pillar tomb (left) tops a grave at the Juma (Friday) Mosque

The people are very friendly, but do remember to ask before you take photographs.

The Juma Mosque, with its pillar tombs, is located near the beach road at the western side of the Old Town, and further east along the beachfront is the tiny Portuguese Chapel, established in the early 16th century. If you feel like a walk, head out on the point to the Vasco da Gama Pillar, the cross on which is reputed to have been brought by the explorer from Lisbon. From here you can get a fine view across to the town and also south to Casuarina Point.

Malindi-Watamu Marine National Park

The park covers about 6 sq km (2¼ sq miles) and is accessed from the park HQ at Casuarina Point south of the town. The Watamu Marine National Park is enclosed by the Malindi Marine National Park and Reserve. With fish well used to snorkellers here (and sometimes even fed by them), it is a good place for beginners to view marine life. For non-snorkellers, glass-bottomed boats are available.

There is no need to book. Just turn up, pay your park fees and you will almost always be spoiled for your choice of boat and skipper. Avoid the period after the long rains in April and May as this is when the water at Malindi has poor visibility, due to the outfall of the nearby Sabaki (Galana) River.

ⓐ Park HQ Casuarina Point 🕐 06.00–18.00 daily ❶ Admission charge

Marafa Depression

About 30 km (19 miles) north-west of the town is an extraordinary physical feature – a sandstone ridge that has been eroded over thousands of years into vivid orange, pink and red gorges and gullies, which look especially beautiful during sunset. The best way to visit is to negotiate a taxi deal through your hotel. Alternatively hire a 4 x 4 vehicle with a driver. The only accommodation available is the basic Marafa Hell's Kitchen Guesthouse with shared facilities, but it is quite easy to do the return trip in a morning or afternoon from Malindi.

MATATUS

Matatus are minibus taxis used extensively by local people to travel around. Although regulations were brought in a few years ago to try and curb overcrowding, speeding and other dangerous or illegal practices related to their operation, tourists are advised not to use them, unless they want a thoroughly 'ethnic' experience – and are willing to take their lives in their hands to boot. They are usually poorly maintained, are very badly driven, and they are the main cause of Kenya's awful road accident figures.

Watersports

A great place for all watersports, especially from May to October, when the water quality is best. **Surfing** is good at certain times, but especially from July to September, when the waves are driven by the Kaskazi wind from the north-east.

TAKING A BREAK

Though most visitors will probably eat in their hotel, Malindi does have a good selection of bars and restaurants, many with a distinct Italian flavour. Whatever their ethnic bent, almost all of them specialise in seafood, which is excellent along the entire Kenya Coast.

Cafés & restaurants

Bahari Fast Food £ ❶   Based in central Malindi, this place is popular with budget travellers, serving good-quality cheap food. ➋ Off Mama Ngina Street near Juma Mosque ❶ Cash only

Palantine Tea Room £ ❷   If you need to keep up with European football whilst on holiday, this is the place to go, with a mix of food styles, disco and satellite TV. ➋ Mama Ngina Street ❸ 042 31412 ❶ Cash only

◆ *The 15th-century Vasco da Gama Pillar marks the northern end of Casuarina Beach*

🔺 *Driftwood, one of the coast's oldest hotels*

Baby Marrow ££ ❸ Excellent but pricey range of seafood and steaks. ⓐ Silversands Road ⓣ 0733 542584 ⓘ Accepts credit cards

Baobab ££ ❹ A beach bar-café that is a favourite with both travellers and the expat community. Cheerful service and a nice range of seafood, steaks and Italian dishes. ⓐ Silversands ⓣ 042 31699 ⓘ Cash only

Coral Key Beach Restaurant ££ ❺ Specialises chiefly in Italian and seafood but also *nyama choma* (literally 'burnt meat', which is the Swahili for barbecue). ⓐ Silversands ⓣ 042 30717 ⓦ www.coralkeymalindi.com ⓘ Accepts credit cards

Driftwood ££ ❻ Some of the tastiest food in town, and good value too. Try the Friday night barbecue and the traditional Sunday curry lunch. Eat beside the pool. ⓐ South end of Silversands Road ⓣ 042 30569 ⓘ Accepts credit cards

I Love Pizza ££ ❼ Located just opposite the fishing club. Good pasta, pizzas and seafood. ⓐ Silversands ⓣ 042 20672 ⓘ Accepts credit cards

Surahi ££ ❽ If you like Indian food, this is the place to go in Malindi: it's extremely high quality. Dishes include rogan josh and mutton chilli masala, and there is a good range of fish and also vegetarian options. ⓐ Mtangani Road ⓣ 042 30452 ⓘ Accepts credit cards

Casino Malindi £££ ❾ Casino Malindi also has one of the best restaurants in town, inevitably catering for its main clients, the expatriate and visiting Italian community. ⓐ Lamu Road ⓣ 042 330878 ⓘ Accepts credit cards

Lorenzos £££ ❿ Undoubtedly the classiest place to eat in town, this has a lovely ambience which evokes a 'wow' response; it is not very 'Malindi', though. Excellent food, mainly Italian. ⓐ At Mwembe Resort, off Lamu Road ⓣ 042 31758 ⓘ Accepts credit cards

Old Man and the Sea £££ ⑪ This seafront restaurant specialises in upmarket seafood and steaks. Its name is taken from the title of one of Ernest Hemingway's best-known works, and recalls the American author's association with Malindi. ⓐ Silversands ⓣ 042 31106 ❶ Accepts credit cards

THE SWAHILI CULTURE

Most of us tend to think of Swahili as a language, but in fact it is much more. Swahili culture is a result of over 2,000 years of trading around the Indian Ocean, involving Arabs, Persians, Indians and Bantus (Africans). The mix of languages this produced is called Kiswahili, and the religion the Swahili people adopted is Muslim. From Mogadishu in Somalia to the Ruvuma River in Mozambique, we find the same people, the same way of living and the same language.

Earliest descriptions of the culture come from Greek traders in the 2nd century AD. Muslims arrived in the 8th century, and tradition describes Sultan Ali bin Seleimani, from Shiraz in Persia, marrying the daughter of the African headman Mrimba, from Kilwa.

The Swahilis have been mainly city and town dwellers, creating over the centuries the great trading centres of Zanzibar, Lamu, Mombasa and Malindi. In addition a whole succession of thriving towns such as Gedi, Takwa and Kilwa have mysteriously been abandoned during the last 300 years. One theory is that the water supply failed and that wells ran dry. More likely is that the original inhabitants were displaced by the warlike and expansionist Oromo-speaking (Galla) tribe from the north.

It is ironic that Vasco da Gama, credited with establishing the first passage from Europe to the Far East, in 1498 actually hired a navigator at Malindi to take him on the trade route that had already been in use by the Swahilis for at least 1,500 years.

AFTER DARK

Bars, discos & casinos

Unlike Lamu, partly because there are more Italians living in the area, Malindi does have a nightlife.

The Beer Garden ⑫ The clue's in the name: a late-night beer garden and eating place. Stays open until the last customer leaves. ⓐ Located on Lamu Road ❶ Cash only

Casino Malindi ⑬ Long-time established casino, with mainly Italian clients. Play, eat and drink all night long, or at least until 05.00. ⓐ Lamu Road ❶ 042 30878 ❶ Accepts credit cards

Chic Restaurant ⑭ Despite its title, this is actually a beer garden with food and African music. Open until midnight ⓐ Off Tsavo Road on south side of town ❶ Cash only

Club 28 ⑮ A small nightclub playing local music. ⓐ Lamu Road ❶ Cash only

Fermenta Disco ⑯ Italian bar playing European music and hosting karaoke. ⓐ Galana Centre ❶ Cash only

Stardust ⑰ The most popular disco-bar-club in town. Often very crowded. ⓐ Lamu Road ❶ Cash only

A WARNING

It is worthwhile reminding visitors that Kenya does have a serious problem with HIV/AIDS. Men visiting bars and discos *will* be approached by prostitutes, many of whom will be infected with the virus. **It is simply not worth taking the risk.**

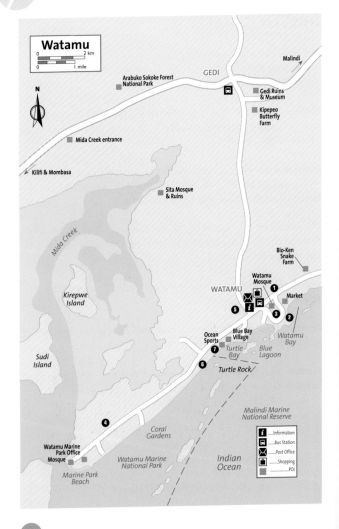

Watamu

0 — 2 km
0 — 1 mile

Malindi

GEDI

Arabuko Sokoke Forest
National Park

Gedi Ruins
& Museum

Kipepeo
Butterfly
Farm

N

Mida Creek entrance

Kilifi & Mombasa

Sita Mosque
& Ruins

Mida Creek

Bio-Ken
Snake
Farm

Kirepwe
Island

Watamu
Mosque

WATAMU

❶

Market

❺

❸

❷

Ocean
Sports

Blue Bay
Village

Watamu
Bay

❼

Turtle
Bay

Blue
Lagoon

Sudi
Island

❻

Turtle Rock

❹

Malindi Marine
National Reserve

Coral
Gardens

Watamu Marine
Park Office
Mosque

Watamu Marine
National Park

Indian
Ocean

Marine Park
Beach

i	Information
🚌	Bus Station
✉	Post Office
🛍	Shopping
■	POI

Watamu

Only in the last 20 years has Watamu grown to become one of the world's top locations for deep-sea game fishing, and one of the best places on the Kenya Coast to dive and snorkel.

Watamu village, adjacent to the resort hotels, is small and still developing. There are a few bars, restaurants and shops, together with curio sellers, but in general there is not much to distract holidaymakers from the main business of their beach holiday.

In some ratings, Turtle Bay Beach at Watamu comes out as one of the top ten beaches in the world. It is truly stunning: a swathe of white coral sand borders a lagoon, flooded twice a day by the incoming tide. Beyond the lagoon is the fringing coral reef and Watamu's Coral Gardens, which is where to find the group of giant coral heads, each with their resident swarms of fish of all colours. Dotted around the bay are small, rugged coral islands, some close to the beach and others further out to sea. The fleet of modern deep-sea fishing boats, all bristling with gear, lies at anchor a couple of hundred metres from the beach.

THINGS TO SEE & DO

Arabuko Sokoke Forest National Park

At some point in your holiday you will welcome the cool environment of Arabuko Sokoke, the largest surviving remnant of the indigenous coastal forest. The easiest way to go is to take a taxi from your resort to the Kenya Wildlife Service HQ just south of the Gedi-Watamu junction on the main coast road. It is normally possible to obtain the services of a ranger without prior booking, and the cost is minimal. Having a ranger will greatly enhance your walk or drive in the forest. You might even spot rare species such as Ader's duiker, a tiny antelope, or the golden-rumped elephant shrew, the animal used in the forest logo. Endangered birds include the Sokoke scops owl and the Sokoke pipit.

ⓐ Just south of Gedi-Watamu junction ☎ 042 12462 🕑 06.00–18.00 daily ❶ Admission charge

Bio-Ken Snake Farm

The snake 'farm' in Watamu village is much more worth visiting than
most, as it is one of Kenya's foremost centres for collecting and breeding
snakes for the production of anti-venom. If you were unfortunate
enough to be bitten by a snake (a very rare event), the anti-venom would
likely come from here. Royjan Taylor and his staff will show you a wide
range of snakes and explain how anti-venom is produced. It is also possible
to go on snake-collecting safaris (see page 91).

ⓐ Watamu beach road, north end ❶ 042 32303 Ⓦ www.bio-ken.com
🕐 10.00–12.00, 14.00–17.00 daily ❗ Admission charge

Dolphin-, whale- & whale-shark-watching

Sightings are by no means guaranteed, but at some times spotting is
reliable and exciting. Ask at your hotel for details.

Gedi Ruins

Gedi Ruins are one of the most fascinating visitor sites on the Kenya
Coast. Around 500 to 600 years ago, more than 2,000 people lived at
Gedi, a thriving town of houses, palaces and mosques. Suddenly, about
300 years ago, along with numerous other coastal towns, it was totally
abandoned and never resettled. Equally strangely, there is no written
historical record, in either Arabic or Swahili, of Gedi's existence, in spite
of the fact that a wealth of pottery shards in the ruins is testimony to
its trading connections all over the eastern world.

Explanatory theories abound, ranging from a loss of water supply to
attack from the savage Oromo-speaking people (also known as Galla)
from further up the coast. There is much to see, ranging from the
remains of the Great Mosque, the Sultan's palace, numerous pillar
tombs (monumental graves marked with a pillar), and a host of small
mosques, houses and dozens of deep wells. Alongside the ruins is the
much-underused Gedi Museum, which displays a wide range of the
artefacts that have been discovered.

The best way to get there is by taxi from either Watamu or Malindi.
It is also a short enough distance to cycle.

⬥ *The atmospheric and mysterious Gedi Ruins*

ⓐ Close to modern Gedi village, just off the main coast road
🕒 07.00–18.00 daily ❶ Admission charge

Kipepeo Butterfly Farm

At the entrance to the Gedi Ruins you will also find a small community-run butterfly farm (Kipepeo means 'butterfly'). The operation is fairly simple, but visit in the cool of the morning and you will see the butterflies at their most active.
ⓐ Close to modern Gedi village, just off the main coast road
🕒 08.00–17.00 daily ❶ Admission charge

Mida Creek

Mida Creek is the huge inlet just south of Watamu and it is possible to arrange trips into the creek through the mangroves, for bird-watching, and to Sudi Island, in the creek, where there are boardwalks through the mangroves. One commonly sighted bird is the palm nut vulture. Trips to the creek will normally be organised by your hotel: Hemingways, for example, offers a free Mida Creek trip in their normal package.

DEEP-SEA GAME FISHING

The American author Ernest Hemingway came to the coast of Kenya in the 1930s and fell in love with big-game fishing, especially from Malindi and Watamu. At the time there was almost no development at Watamu. Big-game fishing remained a perennial fascination for the novelist: one of Hemingway's last works was *The Old Man and the Sea* (1952), a novella about a Cuban fisherman's epic struggle with a giant marlin. Since 1988, **Hemingways Resort** has grown up both to commemorate and to celebrate Hemingway's way of life here. Watamu is now a world-famous location for fishing for big-game billfish.

Nowadays, bobbing at anchor are a dozen or so highly equipped boats, waiting for their twin engines to race them out to the offshore fishing grounds. Each has fish-finders and ultra-modern fishing gear. The main species of prey sought are sailfish, swordfish, various marlin – and a whole range of other species, including sharks. In an effort to ensure continued survival of these extraordinary creatures, most fish are now tagged and returned to the sea, though you can usually pose for a photograph with your catch before it swims off. The season extends from August through the northern hemisphere winter to April.

Inevitably this is an expensive add-on to your trip, ranging from about £200 for a half day (five hours) to over £500 for a full day (ten hours) depending on the season and size of boat. Bookings can be made at your hotel.

Watamu Marine National Park

Established in 1968, and now part of a UN World Biosphere Reserve, this marine park has over 150 species of both hard and soft corals and a host of spectacular and colourful fish species as well as green and hawksbill turtles.
☎ 042 32393 ⏱ 06.00–18.00 daily ❶ Admission charge

🔺 *Man versus black marlin: these days the fish usually wins*

Watersports
Diving
This is one of the best dive locations on the Kenya Coast. Watamu has three PADI-registered diving schools (Aqua Ventures at Ocean Sports ☎ 042 32420, Hemingways ☎ 042 32624, and Turtle Bay Beach Club ☎ 042 32003), with the national park and the coral gardens just offshore. There are about 20 recognised dive sites, usually only 10–20 minutes from the beach.

The best season is October to April, when visibility is normally 15–40 m (50–130 ft). During the period October to April, the appearance of krill also attracts the huge whale sharks and manta rays to the area. During June to November, look out for humpback whales.

⬣ *Palm trees and pure sands on Watamu beach*

Snorkelling

Snorkelling is one of the most popular activities and there are many possibilities for hiring gear, at the National Park HQ or from your hotel. For the first-time snorkeller the experience can be simply awesome, with the most amazing collection of different-shaped and coloured fish. But beware. It is extremely easy to get sunburned when snorkelling. Make sure you have ample, high-factor sun-block, especially on the backs of your arms and legs, particularly the top of your legs where the skin will be exposed as you dive downwards. And wear a T-shirt in the water.

Waterskiing & other watersports

A full range of watersports is available, including sailing, waterskiing, jet-skiing, parasailing, and most recently kite-surfing. Ask at your hotel for details on what is available.

CORAL REEFS

Coral reefs are structures produced by living organisms. They occur in warm seas, mainly on the east coast of continents between 30 degrees north and south of the equator. Coral needs clear, unpolluted water, and so disappears at the mouths of rivers such as the Sabaki, north of Malindi. Commonest are the stony corals, which produce an external skeleton of limestone. Reefs form only in shallow water, where sunlight can penetrate.

At present the world's coral reefs are seen to be under threat, either from pollution, or the effects of global warming; coral is especially sensitive to changes in water temperature. At present rates of destruction it is possible that 70 per cent of coral could be gone in 50 years. Though National Park status protects some areas from fishing and trophy hunters, and there are strict guidelines to protect coral from damage by divers and snorkellers, the general threat remains.

TAKING A BREAK

Cafés & restaurants

There is a vibrant though limited local scene, where you can find something different and meet an alternative crowd from those in the resort. Places selling alcohol normally do food as well. Though Watamu is not regarded as an especially unsafe area after dark, it is nevertheless better to take a taxi.

Choma Village Restaurant £ ❶ Cheap and cheerful barbecue. ⓐ Located at the northern edge of Watamu village. ❶ 042 32198 ❶ Cash only

Coolers £ ❷ Simple café specialising in juices, ice creams and shakes. ⓐ Watamu village, opposite Ascot Hotel ❶ 042 32288 ❶ Cash only

Ascot Hotel ££ ❸ Good-quality Italian food, especially pizzas, with sensibly priced wines (note that many hotels do have extremely inflated wine prices). ⓐ In Watamu village ❶ 042 32326 ❶ Accepts credit cards

Pilli Pan ££ ❹ Seafood and steaks. ⓐ South of Watamu on Mida Creek ❶ 0736 724099 ◕ Daily except Mondays ❶ Accepts credit cards

Scary McNasty's ££ ❺ This is a new place that is all the rage with the locals. A bar and grill, specialising in very large portions. Flagship meal is a monster T-bone steak. ⓐ Gedi Road, next to the post office ❶ 042 32500 ❶ Accepts credit cards

Turtle Bay Beach Club ££ ❻ The Turtle Bay pizzeria is popular with locals. ⓐ Watamu waterfront ❶ 042 32003 ❶ Accepts credit cards

Hemingways £££ ❼ Still a popular place to eat and drink with locals, with a wide-ranging menu, especially seafood. Surprisingly, the best-priced house wine on the Kenya Coast. ⓐ Watamu waterfront ❶ 042 32624 ❶ Accepts credit cards

Kilifi

Twenty years ago, Kilifi's economy depended on its location at the northern end of the short ferry crossing across Kilifi Creek, but then a bridge was built, and the town suffered something of a recession. However, Kilifi is an attractive alternative to the other, busier resorts: it is ultra-quiet and is a favoured mooring point for wealthy boat-owners from all over the world. Those who can afford to live there are drawn by its lack of development.

BEACHES

Kilifi beaches are really only accessible from a few hotels, principally Kilifi Bay Beach Resort and Mnarani Club, which have the usual palm-fringed coral-sand beaches, with the reef a few hundred metres offshore, plus all the usual water activities available.

THINGS TO SEE & DO

Dhow trips

Dhow trips in the creek are bookable through your hotel.

Kilifi Boatyard

The Kilifi Boatyard, on the south side of the creek, is a good, simple place to enjoy crab samosas while gazing at the sailors who can afford to pay out a million or so pounds or dollars for their 'hobby' boat.
📍 South side of creek. Turn off main road opposite Mnarani Club
📞 041 525067 🌐 www.kilifiboatyard.com

Mnarani Ruins

Situated between the bridge and the boatyard are the Mnarani Ruins. This was another thriving Swahili town, mysteriously abandoned in the 17th century, probably under pressure from the marauding Galla people. Best preserved are the Great Mosque, various carved tombs and a

○ Tranquil Kilifi Creek and the new bridge

16th-century mosque. It also boasts supposedly the biggest baobab tree on the Kenya Coast.

🅐 South Kilifi Creek 🕐 07.00–18.00 ❶ Admission charge

Watersports

Although Kilifi is not thought of as one of the major diving and snorkelling centres, **Mnarani Club** (☎ 041 522318) and **Kilifi Bay Beach Resort** (☎ 041 522264) offer a variety of water-based activities. **Barracuda Diving** are located at Mnarani Hotel, and local reefs include Takaunga, Borfa and Barracuda. The Vuma caves are also an interesting dive.

TAKING A BREAK

Cafés & restaurants
Kilifi Boatyard £ Does excellent, simple crab samosas and fish and chips, within a lovely ambience overlooking all the moored yachts. 🅐 South side of the creek, west of the bridge ☎ 041 525067 ❶ Cash only

Baobab Lodge ££ Traditional coast hotel food. 🅐 Above the beach, west of the town ☎ 041 522570

Kilifi Bay Beach Resort ££ This is the best of Kilifi resort hotels, with a superb ocean-view location and excellent international food. 🅐 Northwest of Kilifi, right on the beach ☎ 041 522264 ❶ Accepts credit cards

Mnarani Club ££ With an entrance just beyond the bridge, the club has a large restaurant overlooking the creek, and serves quite reputable international food. 🅐 South side of Kilifi Creek ☎ 041 522318 ❶ Accepts credit cards

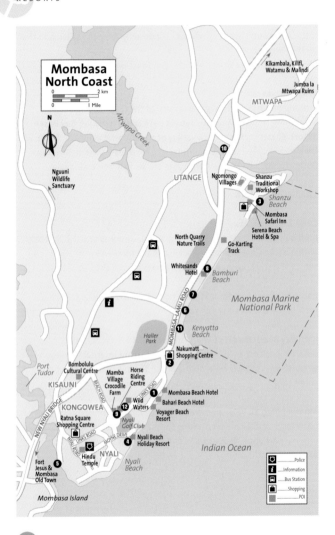

Mombasa North Coast

The Mombasa North Coast is the area between Mombasa Island and Mtwapa Creek. It is the most important resort area on the coast, with over 30 large hotels, almost all enjoying a coral beach and access to the fringing reef. Until the 1960s there was only one hotel, at Nyali Beach, just outside Mombasa Town. Since then a strip of modern hotels, mainly for the European package market, has emerged. Many hotel developers also have safari lodges and camps in the national parks, making it easy to arrange a 'beach' and 'bush' combined holiday.

BEACHES

The beach on Mombasa North Coast is pretty well non-stop white coral sand, backed with coconut palms on the landward side, and with a tidal lagoon between the beach and the fringing reef located a few hundred metres offshore. Most hotels have their own beach area.

The main beach designated as 'public' is the busy Kenyatta Beach, which is accessed from the Mombasa–Lamu Road near the entrance to Haller Park.

THINGS TO SEE & DO

Fort Jesus

Fort Jesus is Mombasa's number one historical visit. Built by the Portuguese, it was actually designed by an Italian. Most spectacular are the restored Omani House, the roof of which gives a great view over Mombasa Town, and the Hall of Mazrui. The Fort Museum has a large collection of pottery, evidence of the earlier trading connections between Mombasa and the rest of the world, especially China.

Fort Jesus is home to a sound and light show, staged every night except Tuesdays and Sundays at 19.30, and organised by different providers. Most romantic is to arrive at Fort Jesus by dhow, enjoy the light show and presentation of the history of the East African coast, and finish with a candlelit dinner within the walls of the fort. The price will depend on the package you choose; these can be booked in your hotel.

Fort Jesus ⓐ South end of Old Town in Makadara ☏ 041 2312839
🕓 08.30–18.00 daily ❶ Admission charge

Fort Jesus Sound & Light Show 🕓 19.30 daily except Tues & Sun
❶ Admission charge

Golf

The Nyali Golf Club course is 5,953 m (6,510 yds), par 71. It is used as a championship course. It has a dress code, so check what you need to wear first. Visitors are welcome.

ⓐ Links Road ☏ 011 471589 🕓 08.00–18.00 ❶ Admission charge

🔺 *Cannons at the ready at 16th-century Fort Jesus*

Haller Park

Haller Park is a fine example of reclamation and conservation, where a former cement quarry has been turned into a wildlife park. Visitors have the chance to stroll through the recreated forest and to experience a wide variety of animals ranging from giraffes to hippos, crocodiles and poisonous snakes.

🕐 08.00–17.00 daily ❶ Admission charge

Jumba la Mtwapa Ruins

The mansion of the slaves is another fascinating example of a Swahili settlement, deserted about 300 years ago. Now a national monument, with a collection of mosques and the house of the wealthy residents.

ⓐ North of Mtwapa Creek 🕐 08.00–18.00 daily

Mamba Village Crocodile Farm

Most visitors can't resist a visit to see Big Daddy, a former man-eating crocodile translocated from the Tana River in 1986, measuring more than 5 m (16 ft) and weighing in at just under a tonne. While you are there, how about trying crocodile meat, which is offered on the menu in the Mamba restaurant?

ⓐ Links Road 🕐 08.00–18.30 daily ❶ Admission charge

Mombasa Old Town

The Old Town is located between Diego Road and Mombasa Creek. A maze of lanes, similar to those in Lamu or Zanzibar, date mainly from the 19th century. Mosques are usually older; the Mandhry Mosque (1570) is the oldest, though the Basheikh Mosque is also described by the local inhabitants as being 'very old'. Suitably dressed men (no shorts) may enter the mosques, but women are not allowed in at all.

Watersports

All hotels along this coast normally have a wide range of watersports on offer, including jet-skiing, banana-boats, waterskiing, windsurfing, canoeing and kite-surfing. Some are obviously dependent on the tide,

⏺ *Have a splashing day at Wild Waters, Nyali*

which, at its height, twice a day will lap the seaward edges of your resort hotel, and when low will expose about 500 m (1,600 ft) of lagoon and rock pools.

As a rule most visitors use the hotel pool for **swimming**, rather than the sea. However, most of the time it is perfectly safe to bathe in the sea inside the reef. Do remember, though, that this is a Muslim region, and in any case topless or nude bathing or sunbathing are illegal in Kenya. You are also just south of the equator, and serious sunburn is a constant risk at any time of the year, even when the sun only appears hazy. Apply lots of high-factor sun-block and ensure kids are kept covered up.

This is another superb area for **diving** for all levels of expertise, and there are PADI-registered dive schools all along the coast. Apart from the delights of the reef, the area also boasts the best dive-wreck on the East African coast, MV *Dania*, sunk in 2002, and now the home for a host of moray eels, barracudas, groupers, crabs and lobsters.

With the reef so close to shore, **snorkelling** is the simplest way to experience the wealth of underwater wildlife available. There are also glass-bottomed boats, though the view is sometimes a bit limited. If you snorkel in the National Park, even just from your hotel, you are liable to pay the US$10 park fees.

Wild Waters

A modern, all-action water park with an enormous range of water slides and pools, a games area and 'rain dancing'. Just the thing to keep the young and the young-at-heart amused for the afternoon.
ⓐ Links Road ❶ 041 470408 ⓦ www.wildwaterskenya.com
🕒 11.00–22.00 Mon–Fri, 10.00–22.00 Sat & Sun ❶ Water slides open only until 18.00

TAKING A BREAK

Most guests tend to eat in their resort hotel, but there is a host of places to eat, drink and go clubbing on Mombasa Island and between Mombasa and Mtwapa Creek, mostly used by local residents. This is a small selection of what's on offer.

Misino Restaurant ££ ❶ Authentic Japanese food, including sushi, sashimi and tepanyaki. Considering the quality, surprisingly inexpensive.
ⓐ Near Bahari Beach Hotel, Nyali ❶ 041 471454 ❶ Accepts credit cards

La Veranda ££ ❷ A casual Italian restaurant with good home cooking.
ⓐ Located near Nyali Nakumatt ❶ 041 5485074 ❶ Accepts credit cards

Jehazi Grill £££ ❸ New seafood grill located almost on the beach.
One of the best restaurants on the Kenya Coast. ⓐ Serena Beach Hotel, Shanzu Beach ❶ 020 354771 ❶ Accepts credit cards

🔺 *Tamarind dhow all set for dinner*

Mvita Grill £££ ❹ Located at Nyali Beach Hotel and one of the gems of the north coast. Long-established jazz trio. Gourmet international food. Pricey but very nice. ⓐ Nyali ☏ 011 472325 ❶ Accept credit cards

Tamarind restaurant & dhows £££ ❺ This land-based restaurant has an idyllic location, high on the cliff, overlooking Mombasa Creek and the Old Town, and if you choose to eat on one of their dhows, you will slowly sail around Mombasa Island for three or four memorable hours. It's fairly expensive, with dinner on the dhow costing US$70 a head, but could be the romantic highlight of your holiday, and you will certainly enjoy a gastronomic treat. ⓐ Cement Silo road, between Lamu Road and Links Road ⓣ 041 4744600 ❶ Accepts credit cards

AFTER DARK

Clubs & discos

Pirates £ ❻ The main public beach on the north coast, this also has a beach disco and bar and a stage for live bands. The place to go for *nyama choma* and dancing in the sand. ⓐ Located on Lamu Road near Haller Park ⓣ 041 5486020 ❶ Cash only

Bora Bora ££ ❼ Good mixture of European and African food. ⓐ Ocean View Plaza, Lamu Road ⓣ 041 5486421 ❶ Accepts credit cards

Il Covo ££ ❽ Good Italian and seafood, sushi and tepanyaki. Also operates as a nightclub. ⓐ Near Whitesands on Lamu Road ⓣ 041 548809 ❶ Accepts credit cards

Mamba Village International Night Club ££ ❾ Popular disco at the crocodile farm which is also a scene for local bands. ⓐ Links Road ⓣ 041 475180 ❶ Cash only

Moorings ££ ❿ A floating bar-restaurant, with disco and nice food. Combine your visit with a dhow trip. ⓐ Mtwapa Creek ⓣ 041 5485045 ❶ Accepts credit cards

Tembo Disco ££ ⓫ Garden bar and restaurant, with a wide range of African music. ⓐ Opposite Haller Park, Lamu Road ⓣ 041 5485078 ❶ Cash only

Wild Waters ££ ⓬ Something different for when the heat is getting to you, get thoroughly soaked in a 'rain dance disco'. ⓐ Links Road ⓣ 041 470408 ⓦ www.wildwaterskenya.com ⓛ After 20.00 Fri & Sat ❶ Cash only

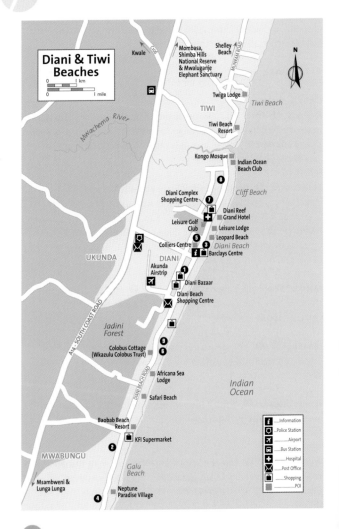

Diani & Tiwi Beaches

0 — 1 km
0 — 1 mile

Kwale

Mombasa, Shimba Hills National Reserve & Mwaluganje Elephant Sanctuary

Shelley Beach

Twiga Lodge

TIWI

Tiwi Beach

Mwachema River

Tiwi Beach Resort

Kongo Mosque

Indian Ocean Beach Club

Cliff Beach

Diani Complex Shopping Centre

Diani Reef Grand Hotel

Leisure Golf Club

Leisure Lodge

Leopard Beach

Colliers Centre

Diani Beach

UKUNDA

DIANI

Barclays Centre

Akunda Airstrip

Diani Bazaar

Diani Beach Shopping Centre

Jadini Forest

Indian Ocean

Colobus Cottage (Wkazulu Colobus Trust)

Africana Sea Lodge

Safari Beach

Baobab Beach Resort

KFI Supermarket

MWABUNGU

Galu Beach

Msambweni & Lunga Lunga

Neptune Paradise Village

A14 - SOUTH COAST ROAD

DIANI BEACH ROAD

C106

MWANEAR ROAD

	Information
	Police Station
	Airport
	Bus Station
	Hospital
	Post Office
	Shopping
	POI

Diani & Tiwi Beaches

Diani and Tiwi are both purpose-built resorts, half an hour south of Mombasa, constructed over the last 30 years, and giving a high standard of accommodation and visitor facilities.

Diani is the more developed, with many hotels, and a good surfaced road accessing the resorts. Tiwi is relatively undeveloped, with a *murram* (dirt) road from the main coast highway, and with no other facilities other than the resorts.

The arrival point for both is via the busy Likoni ferry, which links Mombasa Island with the south coast. South of the ferry, as the road leaves Likoni, it passes through a slum area typical of modern African cities. There is a small airstrip at Ukunda, next to Diani Beach, which is used especially by visitors who include a safari as part of their holiday.

BEACHES

All hotels are built on the beach, which is palm-fringed almost everywhere; the coral reef lies about 500 to 1,000 m (1,600 to 3,280 ft) offshore and there is a lagoon between. The lagoon is tidal, filling and emptying twice a day, but provides lovely swimming and watersports possibilities.

Though it is difficult here to find your own personal beach paradise, an hour down the coast is **Mwazaro Mangrove Lodge** (ⓦ www.keniabeach.com), where you can enjoy palms and coral sand almost on your own. All the resorts also have their own pools, often more than one, and provide a range of water facilities.

THINGS TO SEE & DO

Bike hire

As with Watamu, the totally flat landscape makes this wonderful biking country, so long as you keep a lookout for the dreadful Kenya driving. Bike hire is available from a number of outlets in Diani, and is best arranged through your hotel.

RESORTS

🔺 *Bliss on the beach at Diani*

Dhow trips

A trip in a traditional dhow, whether under sail or motorised, will be a highlight of any visit to Kenya, and a number of companies in the area offer a range of trips, mainly to **Wasini Island** or to savour the delights of the **Kisite-Mpunguti Marine National Park**, reckoned by many divers to be the second best dive site in the world after the Great Barrier Reef.

Dhow trips offer several possibilities, including the usual diving and snorkelling, but also dolphin-watching and, perhaps the most exciting, the chance to view and get close to the world's biggest fish, whale sharks, which regularly visit the Kenya Coast.

The **Pilli Pipa Dolphin Safari** has a booking office at Colliers Centre, Diani Beach. The dhow departs from Shimoni but there are pickups from hotels all along the coast.

ⓐ Behind La Fontanella at Colliers Centre ☏ 041 3202401

ⓦ www.pillipipa.com

Golf

Diani has a fine 18-hole, par-72 championship golf course, run by Leisure Lodge. The course has fully irrigated fairways, a driving range and caddy-carts and it is home to the major competition on the Kenya Coast, the Diani Masters.

ⓐ Leisure Lodge Beach and Golf Resort, Diani Beach Road

☏ 040 3203624 ❗ Credit cards accepted

Jadini Forest

Just south of Diani, at the southern end of the Diani Beach paved road, is Jadini Forest, home to the Wkazulu Colobus Trust, which is wild enough to be home to the world's largest group of Angolan black and white Colobus monkeys. With them are yellow baboons and the bold grey and white Sykes monkeys.

ⓐ Colobus Cottage, south of Diani ☏ 040 3203519

ⓦ www.colobustrust.org 🕐 08.00–13.00, 14.00–17.00 Mon–Sat, closed Sun ❗ Admission charge for guided tours

Mwaluganje Elephant Sanctuary

The Mwaluganje Elephant Sanctuary is only half an hour from Diani, about 15 km (9¼ miles) beyond the Shimba Hills National Reserve entrance, and is well worth a visit. Go in the morning, and have lunch at the **Travellers Elephant Camp**, getting close to elephants as they visit the camp waterhole.

The sanctuary was set up to try and avoid the conflict that previously existed between the needs of local Duruma farmers and those of the hungry, marauding elephants. The local farmers have donated land and in return they enjoy all the benefits that tourism brings. You will almost certainly see a good number of elephants, and the people on the staff are amazingly welcoming.

🕻 0722 343050 ❶ Admission charge

Quad biking

Quad biking is available from Diani village, with packages ranging from half a day in the local forests up to two days in the Shimba Hills.
ⓐ African Quads, South Diani Beach Road 🕻 0721 459258 or 0722 327442

Shimba Hills National Reserve

Shimba Hills is the nearest land-based national park to the coast, and the only one that can be easily visited in a one-day excursion. It is located only half an hour from Diani and Tiwi, and about one hour from Mombasa. It is best to go with a 4-wheel-drive vehicle.

You are unlikely to see any of the big cats (though there are elusive leopards), but you will most likely see elephants, impala, possibly giraffes, and – if you're lucky – the rare sable antelope.
🕻 040 2104259 🕐 06.00–19.00 daily ❶ Admission charge

Trips to Mombasa

Mombasa is about 30 minutes away, plus the time for the ferry, and will give you an experience quite different from just being in your resort. Check in the Mombasa North Coast section (see page 49) for the range of possibilities.

🔺 *Elephants at Shimba*

Watersports
Diving trips

The main companies operate out of Diani and/or the main hotels, and concentrate on Kisite-Mpunguti Marine National Park, usually leaving from Shimoni.

It is important, for your own safety, that you use a reputable company, registered through PADI (Professional Association of Diving Instructors), BSAC (British Sub-Aqua Accreditation) or SSI (Scuba Schools International). Reliable dive companies include:

Charlie Claw's. Based on Wasini Island. Ensures you a great lunch (see page 66). ☎ 040 3202331 & 3203055

Diani Marine ☎ 040 3202367

Your hotel will have all the necessary booking information.

Other watersports

The reef between beach and lagoon provides a great wave-free location for windsurfing, and more recently kite-surfing, which are generally available at all resorts. Parasailing behind a speed boat is also very popular.

With the reef just offshore, snorkelling is probably the most popular activity. The coral literally swarms with a mass of fishes of different shapes and colours. But always remember to protect against the severe tropical sun. Wear a T-shirt, together with lots of high-factor sun-block on vulnerable places such as your arms, legs and the back of your neck.

In addition to these, other watersports are also available, including canoeing, jet-skiing, waterskiing and banana-boats.

TAKING A BREAK

Cafés & restaurants

Self-caterers will often eat out, and on the Diani Beach Road 'strip' there is a developing collection of cafés and restaurants, often of good quality. Though it is probably safe to walk around Diani at night, it is generally advised that you take a taxi.

Locations are described relative to the junction of the link road from the main coast road to the Diani Beach Road.

Riziki Kwa Munga Cafeteria £ ❶ Just south of the junction. Serves cheap, cheerful but good-quality local food. Not somewhere you might go out to for dinner, but a place to try something authentically Kenyan. ⓐ Diani Beach Road, south ❗ Cash only

Sundowner £ ❷ Another very cheap local restaurant at the southern end of the resort strip, where you can sample the range of seafood that Kenyans enjoy. ⓐ Diani Beach Road, south end ❗ Cash only

African Pot ££ ❸ A favourite venue for expats in Diani, as well as restaurant and hotel owners. Serves good-quality, cheap African-style food. ⓐ North Diani Beach Road ☎ 040 3203890 ❗ Cash only

Boko Boko ££ ④ Located at the southern end of the beach, Boko Boko provides something different, a traditional Seychellois restaurant, serving spicy food in a garden atmosphere. Well priced, good value. ⓐ Diani Beach Road, south ⓣ 040 3202344 ❶ Accepts credit cards

La Fontanella ££ ⑤ Located in a mini-version of London's Millennium Dome, at Colliers Centre, north of the junction. Smart modern ambience. Excellent Italian food and coffee. A popular hangout for local Europeans. ⓐ Colliers Centre ❶ Cash only

Forty Thieves Beach Bar and Restaurant ££ ⑥ A beach bar with a disco on Wednesday, Friday and Saturday. It also features live bands and shows English Premier League football. If you feel homesick, this might be the place for you. Same management as Ali Barbour. ⓐ On the beach, south of the Diani Road junction ⓣ 040 3202033 ❶ Accepts credit cards

Galaxy ££ ⑦ Good-quality Chinese restaurant, located in Diani Complex Shopping Centre, north of the Diani Beach Road junction. Nice food; good reputation. Collects from hotels. ⓐ Diani Complex Shopping Centre ⓣ 040 3300018 ❶ Accepts credit cards

Green Palms Bar ££ ⑧ Popular drinking place and eating place with a pool, located north of the junction in Diani Palm Hotel. ⓐ Diani Palm Hotel ⓣ 040 3202523 ❶ Accepts credit cards

Ali Barbour's Cave £££ ⑨ Eating here is a memorable experience. The restaurant is housed in a coral cave and produces a high-quality mixture of seafood and French cuisine. ⓐ On the beach, south of the Diani Road junction ⓣ 040 3202033 ❶ Accepts credit cards

Wasini Island & Shimoni

Wasini Island is located off the extreme southern coast of Kenya.
It is tiny, only about 1 km by 5 km (½ mile by 3 miles), and is totally
undeveloped, with no roads, no cars and very little fresh water. But
offshore it has the Kisite-Mpunguti Marine National Park, which
provides some of the best diving and snorkelling on the coast.

Shimoni is a small, friendly, historic fishing village, at the end of a
17-km (10½-mile) *murram* (dirt) road, which provides the ferry-point
across to the island.

BEACHES

The main beach is Mwazaro, accessed off the dirt road between the
main coast highway and Shimoni. It lies just south of the mouth of the
Ramisi River and the large areas of mangroves, and offers a range of
accommodation and camping.

⬤ *Local boatmen at Shimoni will often hire out their dhows*

THINGS TO SEE & DO

Big-game fishing

Boats and facilities are limited, but the area of Pemba Channel, which is just offshore from Shimoni, provides some of the best fishing waters in the world, especially for marlin and shark.

Pemba Channel Lodge 📞 0722 205020 🌐 www.pembachannel.com
Simoni Reef Lodge 📞 040 52015 ✉ oes@africaonline.co.ke

Dhow trips

As you arrive in Shimoni, you will immediately be assaulted by a mass of young men who want to take you to Wasini, or on a dhow trip. It is all rather hectic, but once the haggling over hire costs is over, peacefully and almost silently cruising the Wasini Channel, especially at sunset, can be an idyllic experience.

Kisite-Mpunguti Marine National Park

The Kenya Wildlife Service HQ is located not far west of Shimoni village and has a small eco-exhibition on the area. Unless you are staying at Shimoni, it is likely that you will arrange diving or snorkelling at Wasini through your hotel, or through one of the companies operating in the shopping centres at Diani. There are several PADI-registered companies (it is most important to ensure they are properly accredited) and a whole-day package is the easiest arrangement.

The park is reckoned to be one of the best unspoiled dive and snorkelling sites in Kenya, and hence in the world. Full-day dhow trips take you to **Mpunguti ya Chini** and **Mpunguti ya Juu** at **Kisite Islet**, where you can reliably enjoy excellent water visibility and a huge range of corals, fish and other sea life. Another good area is **Maki Koke Reef**.
🅰 National Park HQ 📞 040 52027 🕐 06.00–18.00 daily

Shimoni Caves

Shimoni village is small and fairly scruffy but characterful and friendly. One of the sights worth a visit here are its caves, located near the jetty.

They were made famous in the 1980s by their use as the recording venue by Roger Whittaker for his song 'Shimoni'. The caves are believed to have been used as a store for slaves en route to Zanzibar and are now in the charge of National Museums of Kenya. Still not fully explored, they are believed to extend for 5 km (3 miles) or more, and are home to six different species of bats together with a mass of creepy-crawlies.
ⓐ Shimoni village ⓛ 08.30–10.30, 13.30–18.00 ⓵ Admission charge

TAKING A BREAK

Cafés & restaurants
Smugglers £ Does *nyama choma* (chicken, beef and goat) and good breakfasts. ⓐ Just beyond Shimoni Caves ⓵ Cash only

Charlie Claw's ££ Specialises in Swahili-style dishes, especially seafood. Standard lunch menu includes marinated fish in lime juice and steamed whole crab in ginger. ⓐ North Wasini Island ⓣ 040 320331 & 3203055 ⓵ Accepts credit cards

Mpunguti Lodge ££ Another place specialising in very fresh, locally produced seafood. ⓐ Wasini, opposite Shimoni ⓣ 040 52288 ⓵ Accepts credit cards

Shimoni Reef Hotel ££ In a lovely elevated position overlooking the Wasini Channel. Makes simple fresh seafood dishes. ⓐ East of Shimoni ⓣ 040 52015 ⓔ oes@africaonline.co.ke ⓵ Accepts credit cards

Mwazaro Beach £££ Mwazaro Beach is run by food-writer and cook Hans von Loesch. It is off the beaten track, but a phone call in advance should produce an unusually fine lunch. ⓐ Off dirt road halfway between main highway and Shimoni ⓣ 0722 711476 ⓦ www.keniabeach.com ⓵ Accepts credit cards

ⓞ *View landscape and wildlife from a balloon*

EXCURSIONS
Out & about

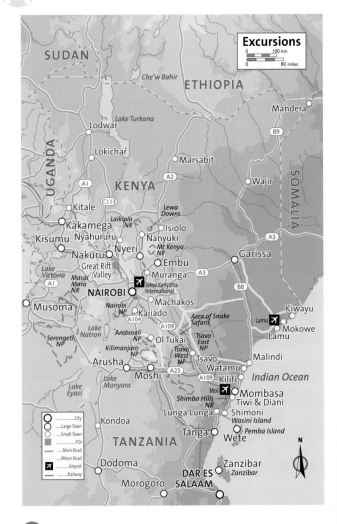

Land & marine safaris

A holiday to the beaches of Kenya is different to most other holiday destinations, because the majority of travellers combine 'beach & bush' and include at least a few days' safari (journey) in one or more of Kenya's incredible wildlife reserves and national parks. You may choose to begin your holiday with a safari or, less commonly, you may start at the beach and end up in the bush. Another way is to choose your safari excursions once you arrive at your destination. All resorts will have a host of possibilities to select from, of which some are listed.

If you want to organise your own customised, upmarket safari, the following companies all offer a specialist service, but be prepared to spend a considerable amount of money:

Abercrombie & Kent 📞 020 334955 🌐 www.abercrombiekent.com
Cheli & Peacock 📞 020 603090 🌐 www.chelipeacock.com
Ker & Downey Safaris 📞 020 891625 🌐 www.kerdowneysafaris.com
Richard Bonham Safaris 📞 020 600457 🌐 www.richardbonhamsafaris.com

THE MARINE SAFARI

The marine safari elevates the short diving or snorkelling trip to one of several days and may even extend beyond Kenyan waters to the islands and coast of Tanzania. There are different options. You can live aboard a sailing yacht for a few days, and visit Shimoni, Pemba, Tanga and Zanzibar. Alternatively it is possible to sail from Shimoni to Pemba and stay there for several days, enjoying the range of diving and snorkelling, with dolphin- and whale-shark-watching available in different locations.

One Earth Safaris are the pioneers of the marine safari and have sea lodges both at Shimoni Reef and at Manta Reef, Pemba, together with a fleet of dive boats and a 23-m (75-ft) live-aboard yacht. Obviously this sort of bespoke tourism is pricey, and at the top end of the market. 📞 041 471771/2 🌐 www.oneearthsafaris.com

Specialist safari airlines include the following:

Air Kenya 📞 020 606539 🌐 www.airkenya.com

Mombasa Air Safari 📞 041 3433061 🌐 www.mombasaairsafari.com

SafariLink 📞 020 600777 🌐 www.safarilink-kenya.com

⬥ *Getting close to elephants*

Masai Mara National Reserve

The Mara, as Kenyans call it, is one of the gems of world wildlife and a 'must' on your safari circuit. If you only do one safari on your holiday, make it the Mara.

The Masai Mara is actually the northern end of the great Serengeti migration system. Many would say it is the best end, where 1.5 million migrating wildebeest and zebra repeatedly have to cross the dreaded, crocodile-infested Mara River, in the never-ending search for fresh grazing. When the migrations are in progress between June and November, they offer one of the world's most enduring wildlife spectacles. Even more dramatic is when up to 10,000 wildebeest cross the Mara River en masse, in the belief that the grass is greener on the other side.

Many in the UK will already be familiar with the area, as home to *Big Cat Diary*, the BBC wildlife programme that follows the fortunes of lions, leopards and cheetahs.

GETTING THERE

It is possible to drive, but presently the road from Nairobi to the Mara is one of the worst in Kenya and not a happy experience. So it is probably best to pay the extra and fly, if you can, which in itself – in a small aircraft – can be a bit of an adventure. Lots of companies provide flights, and Air Kenya, SafariLink and Mombasa Air Safari all have scheduled services (see page 118). During the migration, flying over the vast herds can be totally fascinating.

THINGS TO SEE & DO

Balloon trip

An early morning balloon flight, drifting silently over the stunning landscape and the herds of animals, may well turn out to be the highlight of your holiday. However, it is not cheap – it costs about £200. Balloon trips are bookable at your safari lodge, usually on the evening prior to your flight.

Viewing wildlife from a balloon is an unforgettable experience

Big Cat Diary

Big Cat Diary is the BBC wildlife series that is filmed in the Masai Mara and features families of lions, leopards and cheetahs. The general location used is the north-west, near the Mara River. More specifically, filming of lions usually takes place near the Musiara Swamp, of leopards along the Talek River and of cheetahs at various locations throughout the plains. The base for the filming is a camp near Governors Camp. It is quite normal, at any time of the year, to see presenter Jonathan Scott, long-time photographer in the Masai Mara, working in the area.

Great Migration

The migration of wildebeest, zebras and other smaller animals such as Thomson's gazelle is the world's greatest annual movement of large mammals. It seems to be driven by the variation in rains and pasture, and any time from late June to the end of November you might expect the plains of the Mara to be thronged with hundreds of thousands of wildebeest. Nowhere else in the world can you experience such a population of large plains animals. Staying almost anywhere in the reserve will put you in the path of the migration. There are more than 30 lodges and camps (see page 75).

Lions

Masai Mara has one of the highest lion densities in the world, with about 500 adults. Most famous are the magnificent black-maned males, the rulers of the pride; these prides can be huge, sometimes with over 30 members. The likelihood of seeing large numbers of lions in the Mara, especially with a guide, is very high.

Mara River

The Mara River, from the southern Mara bridge northwards, is the scene for one of nature's most frenetic spectacles. The enormous herds of wildebeest and zebras seem driven, by irresistible forces, to cross the crocodile-infested Mara River, sometimes again and again, in search of pasture. The problem is that the river cuts deeply into its plain and, once

⬥ *Dust clouds always accompany the big herds*

in the water, the animals often find it difficult to get out. Every day the scene is one of chaos and confusion.

The best viewing locations are just to the north of Mara Serena Lodge on the west bank, and south of Governors Camp on the east bank.

Musiara Swamp/Marsh

Musiara Swamp, at the north-west corner of the reserve, is home to the world's most famous group of lions, the Marsh Pride. With water available all year, the swamp forms a magnet for thirsty animals, and therefore a year-round larder for hungry lions. In the Mara this is probably your most reliable place to spot lions – not to mention BBC cameramen and presenters.

STAYING AT MASAI MARA

There are a few high-quality camps and lodges in the reserve, and there are four airstrips serving them. Outside the reserve are more than 20 camps and lodges, mainly of high quality but also including some budget camps, which are served by another six or so airstrips. When you book, check to see the location of your camp or lodge. Although there are probably just as many animals outside the official 'reserve', some visitors can feel a bit miffed to find that their 'Masai Mara safari lodge' is actually some 50 km (30 miles) outside the actual park.

Most camps do two game drives each day, one in the early morning and another in the late afternoon or early evening. Food is almost always superb and there is a variety of evening entertainment, often including Maasai dancing.

Nairobi & Lewa

If you holiday on the beach in Kenya, you will more than likely pass through Nairobi at some stage. So we suggest you make the most of East Africa's number one city, whatever the length of your time here. There is much to do, including a national park right on the doorstep, the best museum in Kenya, and the amazing spectacle of the Great Rift Valley only a short drive away. The nightlife and music scene are vibrant, and the city is the best place to shop in East Africa.

THINGS TO SEE & DO

Carnivore

The number one visitor attraction in Nairobi is more than a restaurant, specialising in an enormous eat-as-much-as-you-like barbecue, which includes crocodile, ostrich and the like, as well as the usual chicken and beefsteak. Definitely not for vegetarians! Others need to experience it at least once.

ⓐ Off Langata Road ⓣ 020 605933 ⓦ www.tamarind.co.ke

David Sheldrick Elephant and Rhino Orphanage

The centre's main job is animal rescue, so there are lots of baby elephants and black rhinos. The centre is another star of TV: it is featured on BBC's *Elephant Diary*.

ⓐ Magadi Road ⓣ 020 891996 ⓦ www.sheldrickwildlifetrust.org
ⓛ 11.00–12.00 daily

Great Rift Valley

Thirty minutes out of the city, on the A10 to Naivasha, you can experience one of the most extraordinary sights in Africa, looking out over the Great Rift Valley, with its floor thousands of metres below. There are several viewpoints that you can stop off at; even the hassle you will get from the curio sellers is worth it.

⬥ Downtown Nairobi skyline

> ## ⓘ WORDS OF CAUTION
> As in most African cities, we recommend you take care in the city centre. Do not walk about with obvious valuables on display, such as expensive watches, jewellery, money-belts, anything ostentatious, and avoid walking around at all after dark. Take taxis even for short journeys.
>
> When you visit bars and clubs, be aware that men will be hassled by prostitutes, and that Kenya still has a very serious issue with HIV and AIDS. By far the most sensible policy is to accept that casual sex is simply not worth the risk.
>
> All visitors to Kenya will be aware of the inter-tribal troubles that followed the December 2007 elections. Though not wishing to minimise the importance of this, it is worth pointing out that the violence was highly localised, generally in Kisumu, Eldoret and in the slum areas of Nairobi. No tourists were involved, and in general none of the main tourist areas – either safari destinations or on the coast – has been affected by the violence.

Karen Blixen Museum

If the tears shed as you watched the film *Out of Africa* are part of your reason for visiting Kenya, visiting Karen Blixen's house – in the area now called Karen – is a must. Much of the film was shot here, and the house gives a good impression of how it would have looked in the early part of the 20th century.

ⓐ Karen Road ⓣ 020 882779 ⓘ Admission charge

Nairobi National Park

Nairobi must be the only capital city in the world bounded by a national park. Home to lions, leopards, rhinos and buffalo, all the 'big five' apart from elephants, here is Africa's wildlife within a stone's throw of the city centre.

Near the entrance is the **Nairobi Safari Walk**, a zoo-type display simulating the range of different habitats that are found in Kenya.

ⓐ Main gate, Langata Road ☎ 020 500622 ⏰ 06.00–19.00 daily
ⓘ Admission charge

National Museum

Rated the best museum by far in Kenya, and located close to most of the city hotels, this covers a wide range of natural history, especially birds and geology. There is good coverage of Kenya as one of the likely homes of mankind, and lovely paintings both of plants and of people by the naturalist and author of *Born Free*, Joy Adamson. If you take in Nairobi before you go to the beach, there is a superb exhibit in the Lamu Gallery on the 'Kenya Coast, 9th to 19th century'.

ⓐ Museum Hill, off Uhuru Highway ⏰ 09.30–18.00 daily ☎ 020 742878
ⓘ Admission charge

Shopping

Nairobi is, without doubt, the best place to shop in East Africa (see page 101).

TAKING A BREAK

Nairobi has literally hundreds of places to eat and drink, covering all tastes and all budgets. In general Westlands, the area just to the west of the city centre, and accessed along Uhuru Highway and Waiyaki Way, is where it all happens. In addition, almost all the main hotels also have a variety of excellent places to eat and drink. Many hotels have lovely poolside restaurants, which are good lunchtime venues. Here is a small selection of popular spots for eating and drinking. Ask at your hotel for advice on the 'in' places to go in the local area.

Restaurants

Garden Square Restaurant £ Cheap African buffet. Live Kenyan music.
ⓐ City Hall Way ☎ 020 226474

Carnivore ££ Nairobi's most famous restaurant, and an iconic visitor experience (see page 76). All-you-can-eat menu, based on exotic meats.

◔ *Ready for diners at Carnivore, Nairobi's number one tourist venue*

Weekend funfair for children. Adjacent is Simba Saloon, one of the most popular live music, eating and drinking venues with the Nairobi young set. ⓐ Off Langata Road ⓣ 020 605933 ⓦ www.tamarind.co.ke

Hong Kong Restaurant ££ First-class Cantonese food. ⓐ Koinange Street ⓣ 020 228612

Java House ££ Number one for breakfast. Very popular coffee shops and eating-houses. A chain located in numerous places around Nairobi, including ⓐ Mama Ngina Street, ABC Plaza and Westlands. ⓣ 020 313564

Kengeles ££ A popular fast-food chain. Good steaks, burgers etc, often with live music in the evening. ⓐ Koinange Street, Langata Road, Lavington and others ⓣ 020 344335

Peppers ££ Steak, fish and chicken. Lovely gardens, welcomes kids. ⓐ Opposite Holiday Inn, Parklands Road ⓣ 020 3755267 ⓔ peppersrestaurant@kenyaweb.com

Moonflower Restauarant £££ Lovely though pricey grills and seafood. Jazz group at weekends. Highly recommended. One of Nairobi's top eating places. ⓐ Kitale Lane, part of Palacina ⓣ 020 2715517

Tamarind £££ Same group as Tamarind, Mombasa, and Carnivore. Mainly expensive, quality seafood, but also pizza and pasta. ⓐ Harambee Avenue ⓣ 020 251811 ⓦ www.tamarind.co.ke

LEWA WILDLIFE CONSERVATION AREA

Lewa is a privately owned wildlife ranch covering over 242 sq km (94 sq miles), and making a valuable contribution to many aspects of wildlife conservation. Its special interest is the protection of rhinos, and the ranch is home to about 10 per cent of Kenya's black rhinos. In addition Lewa has about 15 per cent of the world population of the similarly endangered Grevy zebras. The conservation area occupies a region of breathtaking scenery, with deeply incised plateau steps which fall away to the plains and Maasai steppe to the north.

Lewa is located north of Mount Kenya at the southern edge of the area called Laikipia. Normal access is by air from Wilson Airport in Nairobi. Both Air Kenya and SafariLink have scheduled services.

Immediately to the north is the Maasai group ranch of Il Ngwesi. Not long ago, the same Maasai were hunting lions rather than conserving them. Today they run their own award-winning eco-lodge overlooking the Sirikoi valley. ⓐ Il Ngwesi Group Ranch ⓣ 020 340331

THINGS TO SEE & DO

Greater kudu

Common in South Africa, but rare in Kenya, this is one of the few places where you can see these magnificent animals with their spiral horns.

Grevy zebras

There are only about 4,000 Grevy zebras left (they have finer stripes than the common plains zebra); about 15 per cent of the remaining population are at Lewa. It is ironic that Lewa also has lions, which eat Grevy zebras, though much of their decline can be attributable to human activity, including poaching.

Lewa Swamp

Lewa Swamp is the home to the rare sitatunga, an antelope that lives in water. Though common in and around Lake Victoria, the sitatunga is found in very few other places in Kenya.

Rhino conservation

Lewa is one of Kenya's principal rhino conservation projects and there are more than 80 rhinos, both black and white, in the conservation area. Presently there are over 50 black rhinos, the highest number outside a national park in the country, and about 10 per cent of the entire national population. Getting close to this nervous and endangered animal in the wild will be a real highlight of your trip.

STAYING AT LEWA

Accommodation at Lewa will range from a high-class permanent campsite to luxurious 'home stays' at ranch houses. At all of them you will be pampered. ☎ 064 31405 🔞 www.lewa.org

🔺 *Kenya has only about 500 black rhinos remaining*

Amboseli National Park

Amboseli is many people's favourite, mainly because of its location just to the north of snow-clad Mount Kilimanjaro. The national park exists because of springs that start as rain and snow on the mountain, then percolate into the volcanic rock, to emerge eventually in permanent lakes in Amboseli. Here there is always water, so animals migrate to and fro, to drink, and to feed on the lush swamp vegetation. This is certainly the best place in Kenya to view elephants, because of the reliability of their trips to the water.

🔺 *Kilimanjaro, Africa's highest mountain – your view each morning*

During a visit you will notice the work of researchers from the Amboseli Elephant Trust, the organisation inspired by Dr Cynthia Moss, who has been studying Amboseli elephants for over 30 years; this is the longest-running elephant project in the world. Most famous is Echo, a female featured in a string of TV documentaries (see box below).

All around the park is the land of the Maasai. Although this is a national park, the local cattle herders retain watering rights for their animals, and each day hundreds of cattle are slowly driven to the water from all around.

THINGS TO SEE & DO

Elephant-watching

Getting very close to elephants can be unnerving at first, but one needs to remember that Amboseli elephants have experienced tourists every day of their lives. The important thing is to keep very quiet and to let the elephants do their thing. If you are in the way they will walk around you, often very close. A mother may get a little upset when cut off from her calf, and bulls may be more aggressive when they are in *musth* (when they are more active sexually), but in general Amboseli elephants are very visitor-friendly.

> **ECHO THE ELEPHANT**
>
> Echo is probably the best-known elephant in the world and the subject of numerous documentaries. She has been studied at Amboseli by researcher Cynthia Moss for over 30 years. Echo is now in her late 50s, the matriarch of her family group and not far from the end of her life.
>
> Elephant families are controlled by the dominant (and usually oldest) female, and will be made up of sisters, daughters and immature males. The mature bull elephants live either a solitary life or in small bachelor groups, only rejoining the main family for mating.

It will greatly enhance your experience if you read up a little about elephant social life before your safari, so as to understand more about what is going on.

Maasai

The colour of the cultural landscape you will experience on safari is much affected by the Maasai. They are the people who speak the language 'Maa'. They came to East Africa only about 300 years ago, probably from the Nile valley, and now they occupy land from central Kenya south into central Tanzania. They are traditional cattle herders, and they believe that in the beginning God gave all cattle to the Maasai people. Wealth is still generally measured in cattle.

🔺 *The best place in Africa to view elephants*

⬥ *Maasai woman at a village east of Amboseli*

The Maasai live in villages inside a *boma*, or thorn fence, which protects them especially from lions. Traditionally they migrated with the seasons in search of the best pasture, but now this nomadic way of life is much reduced.

Although most Maasai now go to school, and cattle are inoculated against disease, they are still very vulnerable to the pressures of their environment, especially drought. In early 2006, many lost up to 70 per cent of their cattle. At Amboseli they still depend on the springs for their water supply, and still enjoy watering rights.

You will notice during your safari that the **Amboseli Maasai** still live in a very traditional way, and it is possible to make an organised visit to a local *manyatta* (village). Normally a price is negotiated for a group, and the visit usually includes a welcoming dance, followed by some time in the *manyatta*, meeting the women, followed by the opportunity to buy some craftwork, mainly beads. This is a useful way in which you can make a direct contribution to the people, who often have a very hard life, especially in times of drought.

Observation Hill

Observation Hill, just to the south of the main swamps, provides by far the best viewpoint. It is worth the few hundred metres' trek to the top to look out over the whole of the park, but especially the swamps nearby, with their lush plant growth, when all around it may, at times, be almost desert. Herds of elephants and buffalo are often in the water, with wildebeest and zebras grazing on the better-growing grasses next to the swamps.

Tsavo East and West National Parks

Together Tsavo East and West National Parks constitute the biggest national park area in Kenya, covering over 21,000 sq km (8,000 sq miles). This is the most likely excursion destination for anyone doing a short one- or two-day safari from the coast. It is close enough to come by road and will take only a few hours from Mombasa, a journey recently very much improved.

Tsavo is classical wooded savannah grassland, although both East and West have quite wide variety. Some areas are stunningly beautiful such as Ngulia Mountain, the springs at Mzima, or the expanse of the Galana River as it spreads out south of the Yatta Plateau. The recent lava flows at Shetani volcano are fascinating.

Animal-wise, Tsavo is elephant country. At one stage in the 1960s, before a combination of drought and poaching decimated the herds, there were over 40,000 elephants in the Tsavo eco-system. Today there are only about 8,000.

Tsavo lions are infamous following the 'man-eaters' at Tsavo Bridge: more than a century ago the British started building a railway bridge over the Tsavo River and were routinely attacked by two male lions, who killed – so it was said – up to 135 workers before they were finally shot dead. Tsavo lions are still described by Kenyans as *kali*, meaning aggressive or bad-tempered, probably as a result of the harsh thorn-bush conditions in which they live. So if this is your first safari, to either East or West Tsavo, look out!

THINGS TO SEE & DO

Galana River & Lugard Falls

The Athi River and the Tsavo River combine to form the Galana, and by the time it arrives in Tsavo East National Park it is a sizeable stream. When it spreads out over hundreds of metres, with branching doum palms along its banks, it becomes a strikingly beautiful landscape. At Lugard Falls, the broad river is suddenly channelled through a narrow

⬥ *The magnificent Galana River*

gorge sliced into the rock surface. The enormity of the landscape can be awesome, especially the skies and the sense of space.

Mzima Springs

Number one visit in Tsavo West is this glorious oasis, where underground water from the nearby Chyulu Hills bubbles up to create a beautiful lake of clear water, surrounded by yellow-barked acacia trees.
An underwater viewing chamber allows visitors to inspect the antics of hippos, crocodiles and the hundreds of barbel fish. Mzima is also the water supply for Mombasa.

Ngulia Rhino Sanctuary

The Ngulia Rhino Sanctuary was designed to bring the Tsavo black rhinos back from the verge of extinction. Forty years ago there were perhaps 6,000 rhinos in Tsavo, and today, contained within an electrified fence enclosing about 70 sq km (27 sq miles), there are between 50 and 60 of Kenya's most closely guarded animals. Visitors are allowed access for only two hours each evening, so as not to disturb the animals too much.

Ironically the water, piped in especially for the rhinos, also attracts large herds of elephants, not because of the shortage of water outside the sanctuary, but because elephants love to drink clean water.

SNAKE SAFARI

Many visitors have an unjustified fear relating to snakes. Of course there are snakes in Kenya, but your chances of seeing a snake during a short holiday, never mind being bitten by one, are very small. However, for those with a curiosity about snakes, the snake safari offers an unusual opportunity to get close to these fascinating reptiles.

The Bio-Ken Snake Farm at Watamu (see page 38) runs a series of different snake-spotting and collection expeditions lasting from half a day up to several days. Short trips take place close to Watamu, and longer safaris are normally carried out in the Galana River area, just outside Tsavo East National Park.

The expedition leader is usually Royjan Taylor, probably Kenya's most knowledgeable snake person, and also a Certified Professional Safari Guide.

There are 126 known species of snakes in Kenya, with about 20 per cent of these being seriously poisonous. A snake-hunting trip might find all sorts, from Black Mambas to African Rock Pythons. ☎ 042 32303/0733 290324 ⓦ www.bio-ken.com

◯ Another find on a Galana River safari: a puff adder

Shetani Lavas

In Swahili, Shetani means the devil. Less than 200 years ago the small volcano now called Shetani erupted in northern Tsavo, producing a lava flow several kilometres long, and a series of lava tube caves. Today one can walk on lava flows, which appear to have cooled only yesterday, and explore one of the caves near the volcanic cone. A cinder cone called Chaimu makes a fascinating and relatively easy climb.

ⓘ Both of these activities should only be undertaken with a ranger, as there is the serious possibility of sharing your explorations with elephants, buffalo or even lions.

Viewpoints

There are plenty of easily accessible places in Tsavo from which there are amazing views. Both **Ngulia Lodge** and **Voi Safari Lodge** are located in elevated positions. Ngulia looks out over the Ngulia Rhino Sanctuary, and Voi over a series of waterholes and the enormous expanse of Tsavo East. **Kilaguni Lodge** has probably the best game viewing location. The lodge overlooks a series of manmade waterholes and, during the dry seasons (which exclude November and December and April and May), an almost continuous parade of family groups of elephants come to drink.

> **STAYING AT TSAVO EAST & TSAVO WEST**
> There are many possibilities, from simple and not-so-simple campsites, through to elaborate modern-hotel-type lodges. Most, both in Tsavo East and Tsavo West, are either located at a viewpoint or on a river. Apart from price, your choice will probably depend on whether you want a traditional *Out of Africa* sort of experience, sleeping in a tent (albeit with comfortable beds, hot water and showers), or whether you would prefer something more 'civilised'. Or you can go to somewhere like Finch Hatton's in Tsavo West and enjoy the best of both worlds, with a tent overlooking a hippo pool, and a gourmet dinner accompanied by Mozart's music in the evening.

Shimba Hills National Reserve

Although it is possible to visit Shimba Hills comfortably in one day from Tiwi and Diani Beach, and perhaps also from Mombasa, an overnight stay would be better if you were coming from Malindi or Watamu. The park is accessed from the main coast road south from Mombasa by heading west to Kwale on an excellent road not far from the Likoni ferry.

🔺 *Baby elephants will stay close to their mothers for many years*

At Kwale head straight through the town onto a good *murram* (dirt) road for a short distance to the park main gate.

This is the nearest land-based national park to the coast, and many feel it is much underrated. At only around 300 sq km (116 sq miles), it is small in comparison with Tsavo, or even Masai Mara, but it contains some fascinating wildlife, and its altitude offers an opportunity to escape from the heat of the coast. There are no lions in the park, but you may see leopards, lots of elephants, buffalo, zebras and impala, together with lots of bird-life.

THINGS TO SEE & DO

Sable antelopes
This is the only place in Kenya where you can still see sable antelope. The males are almost black, with white markings, whereas the females are a more chestnut shade.

Sheldrick Falls
The Sheldrick Falls are the most spectacular landscape feature, and you can swim there, or just enjoy a shower from 25 m (82 ft). There are some great viewpoints, especially Pengo Hill (450 m/1,476 ft) from which you can see not only the coast but also the Tsavo and Taita hills.

Accommodation, food and drink are at the Shimba Lodge, built in the style of the original tree lodge, the famous Treetops in the Aberdare National Park, and overlooking a waterhole.

ⓣ 040 2104259 ⓛ 06.00–19.00 ⓘ Admission charge

◗ *Pool, palms and peace at the Serena Beach Hotel*

Food & drink

Eating in Kenya is generally informal. However, many places still have a
dress code – for example, prohibiting swimwear, sportswear, sleeveless
T-shirts and similar for evening dining. Read the information in your
room to avoid any awkwardness.

'Swahili cuisine' may be found all the way down the coast of East
Africa from Lamu in Kenya to Zanzibar and Tanzania. It is a mixture of
all the influences that have affected the coast during hundreds of years:
African, Arabic, Indian and, since 1598, European.

Seafood is especially important, with a wealth of very fresh fish and
shellfish. Pemba and Zanzibar are renowned spice islands, so it is not
surprising the food is spicy. Tropical fruits are much used, from coconuts
and coconut milk to mangoes and paw-paws.

From African tradition comes *nyama choma*, which literally means
'burnt meat', and is what Westerners call barbecued meat. This might
be goat, beef or, most likely today, chicken. *Nyama choma* is one of the
staples of the cheap, roadside café.

Hotels normally do an international range of food, although many,
especially the large resorts, will also have specialist restaurants serving
one or several of a range of cuisines. Breakfast is usually an international
buffet, where you choose what you like from a normally huge range.
Lunch tends to include pizzas, sandwiches of varying kinds and snacks,
often served around the pool. The main meal is dinner, starting at about
19.30–20.00.

Many places do what they call an 'African night', where they serve a
collection of local dishes, as well as other selections. They will have
nyama choma of varying kinds, as well as grilled whole fish, various
stews with meat, beans and peanuts, *irio* (made from potatoes, cabbage
and beans, all mashed together), *ugali* (maize meal made into a solid
porridge, a bit like mashed potato), *matoke* (vegetable banana) and other
African delicacies. Classical Swahili food dishes might feature any local
seafood, cooked with plenty of herbs and spices and perhaps with
coconut milk. If you go fishing, it is most likely that your hotel will be

only too happy to cook your catch for you for dinner on your return. Ask them before you set out.

If you happen to stay at Malindi, be prepared for a cultural and gastronomic surprise. Most of Malindi's large expatriate population are Italian, so almost all restaurant menus are in Italian and English. Some do totally Italian food, and the wines may well be Italian as well.

Vegetarians are well taken care of, especially if they go for Indian cuisine. Several restaurants, especially in Mombasa, specialise in very high-quality Gujarati vegetarian curries, using local vegetables and fruits. You may also have noticed the words 'Produced in Kenya' on many of the packs of vegetables sold in European supermarkets. Most come from the Naivasha area but are available throughout the country. All hotels try to cater well for vegetarians.

Restaurants on the Kenya Coast have a particular penchant for striving for a 'romantic' setting, endeavouring to make sure you really do feel you are in Paradise. In many places candlelit tables, under the moon and overlooking the beach, are the norm, such as at Hemingways, the rooftop restaurants of Lamu or the Friday night barbecue at Driftwood. Others have a stunning view, for example Tamarind, overlooking the Mombasa Creek and the Old Town, or Shimoni Reef Lodge, with its restaurant perched high above the Wasini Channel.

Generally the advice is not to drink the tap water, although it is claimed that Nairobi water is perfectly drinkable. Bottling spring water is a growth industry in Kenya, and numerous brands are available, often supplied free in hotel rooms. It is also important to stay well hydrated in the high coastal temperatures.

Nearly all wines are imported, especially from South Africa. With only a few exceptions hotels do tend to be a little excessive and short-sighted over their mark-up on wines. However, Kenya does produce some well-priced beers and lagers, most famous of which is Tusker.

Tipping in restaurants is normal if you feel you have had service worth rewarding. If service has been poor, there is no need to tip. KSh100–KSh200 would be a reasonable tip for a waiter.

LIFESTYLE

Menu decoder

Almost all menus you come across in Kenya will be in both English and Swahili. However, if you do choose to experiment with visiting small African cafés, you may find this useful. In any case, even if you don't, it will allow you to show off when talking with the waiters in your hotel.

Pronunciation is very simple, and totally phonetic. Assume each vowel is a syllable, so if there are two 'a's together, as in *Kaanga*, pronounce them both, 'ka-anga'. There are no silent letters. Everything is pronounced. Here are some basic words.

Bottle Chupa
Bread Mkate
Coffee Kahawa
Cold Baridi
Eggs Mayaie
Fish Semaki
Food Chakula
Fried Kaanga
Fruit Matunda
Hot Moto
Ice Barafu
Meat Nyama
Milk Mziwa
Pepper Piripiri
Plate Sahani
Salt Chumvi
Spoon Kijoko
Sugar Sukari
Tea Chai
Vegetables Mboga
Water Maji

FROM THE MENU
Irio Mixture of mashed potato, cabbage and beans
Keki Cake
Kondo Lamb
Kuku Chicken
Limau Lime
Mahindi Maize (corn)
Mandazi Similar to doughnut
Marahagwe Red beans
Matoke Vegetable banana, usually boiled and mashed
Maziwalala Yogurt
Mbuzi Goat
Mchele Plain, boiled rice
Michicha Spinach
Mkate mayai Like French toast, bread dipped in egg and fried
Muhogo Cassava, often chips
Mushkaki Kebab

Namasi Pineapple
Nazi Coconut
Ndizi Banana
Ngombe Beef, cattle
Nguruwe Pork
Nyanya Tomatoes
Papai Paw-paw
Pilau Rice with spices and meat
Samosa Triangular wrap around spicy filling either meat or vegetable

Sukuma Wiki Shredded greens, such as kale or spinach
Ugali Staple African food, a sort of solid maize meal porridge, a bit like mashed potato
Uji Millet porridge
Viazi Potato
Vitunguu Onion

Even if you have no need to speak Swahili, you will get a great response if you try saying anything at all beyond the usual *Jambo* and *Hakuna Matata* that many people learned from *The Lion King*!

▲ *Carved warriors and animals make for striking souvenirs*

Shopping

KENYAN SPECIALITIES
Basketware
This is also a speciality of the Akamba tribe, and made in a wide range of materials, from sisal, beadwork, bark, leather as well as in modern synthetic materials.

Beadwork
Best known is the beadwork made by the Maasai, and that of the Samburu from northern Kenya. In Nairobi there are several weekly Maasai markets, each with a massive collection of necklaces and bracelets. Biggest is on Friday at Village Market (see page 104). Maasai dancers at hotels usually finish their dance display by rolling out a selection of beadwork.

Carvings
Carved goods are available everywhere in the country. Most common are those produced by the Akamba people, who are found between Nairobi and Mombasa. The majority are of animals, especially elephants, antelopes and giraffes.

More valued are the carvings of the Makonde people, from southern Tanzania and northern Mozambique. Classically these are carved in the hard black timber ebony, though many modern versions are made from stained rosewood. Makonde carvings may be of several different forms; some show complicated intertwined bodies, whereas others are sinister and depict the devil in various forms.

Masks are widely available but, as there is limited tradition of masks in Kenya, they are most likely to be imports from Central and West Africa.

Soapstone carvings are indigenous, though – they come from Kisii, south of Kisumu on Lake Victoria. The soft stone is carved into a wide range of artefacts, from bowls, plates and boxes to chess sets and candlesticks, often done in vivid colours. Stick to shapes that will not be broken in transit.

LIFESTYLE

Musical instruments

Although it may be difficult to get hold of something that you can actually play, musical instruments make a genuine Kenyan souvenir. Drums, covered in cowhide, are most popular, but there are numerous other items on sale, including lyres and the thumb piano, made from a small resonator box with a selection of reeds of varying lengths.

Textiles

Kenya is the perfect place to buy textiles. *Kikoys* and *kangas*, the flexible wraparounds used by both men and women, come from the coast, but they are available everywhere. When you are on a beach holiday, a *kikoy* makes the ideal garment to wrap yourself in as you come back into your resort. Additionally they make lovely, colourful gifts.

The second major textile souvenir item is the Maasai *shuka*, a tartan-like blanket which now forms part of modern Maasai dress. Thirty years ago the Maasai dressed in ochre-coloured blankets, but during recent years have taken to wearing much more colourful garments. Although this is a recent 'tradition', *shukas* make fine gifts.

Tribal regalia & weapons

Tribal regalia and weapons such as spears, bows, drums and clubs, together with domestic utensils, often come from remote areas in northern Kenya.

Wire toys

Usually sold in the streets, intricately made wire toys, mainly motorbikes, cars and trucks, are very much a Kenyan tradition.

WHERE TO SHOP
Hotels & resorts

Almost all hotels, especially the larger ones, will have a gift shop, usually selling quality souvenir items. If you want to shop in your resort without any hassle this might be the best option for you. But you are likely to be paying top prices.

On the beach, just beyond the resort limits, you will often find a bevy of local traders, selling a range of Kenya souvenirs, especially *kikoys* and *kangas*. Shopping here will offer you a bigger selection, better prices and the opportunity for some fun haggling.

Malindi

Curio sellers in Malindi have been organised into a craft market, located at the northern end of the beach, close to the Old Town. Here you can buy a wide range of goods. Beware of buying shells. You will find them on sale, but you may be breaking the law if you try to take them home. On Lamu Road there are numerous upmarket curio stores, especially at Malindi Arcade.

Mombasa

Mombasa is generally ranked only after Nairobi as the place to shop in Kenya. There is a long tradition of craft and curio shops on Moi Avenue, between the 'Tusks' and the Old Town. Look for Harria's and Labeka for

🔵 *Clothes shop in Malindi*

something special. To check out the local shopping scene, head for the Mackinnon Market and the nearby Old Town streets.

Nairobi

Nairobi is, without doubt, the best place to shop in East Africa, with a huge range of possibilities. There are scores of places to shop in central Nairobi, with the main cluster on Standard Street, Kaunda Street and Mama Ngina Street. Also look for the Zebra Craft Centre on Koiange Street, Batik Heritage on Muindi Mbingu Street and Africa Heritage at Libra House and also at Carnivore.

Community craft centres

There are numerous self-help groups around Nairobi who market their crafts together.

Bega Kwa Bega supports the Korogocho Project in the slums of eastern Nairobi. They form a federation of small craft producers. 📞 020 279 1734 🌐 www.begakwabega.com

Kamili Designs produce local, hand- and screen-printed textiles in Karen. 📍 Langata Road, Karen 📞 020 883640 ✉ info@theafricahouse.com

Kazuri Beads is in Karen, and also at Village Market and the Junction Shopping Centre. The company produce jewellery, beads, ceramics and a range of dinnerware. 📞 020 883500 🌐 www.kazuri.com

Utamaduni Craft Centre is the location for 18 different craft shops. 📍 Bogani Road East 📞 020 891798 🌐 www.utamadunicrafts.com

Maasai markets occur all around the city, but specifically near the Globe Cinema roundabout on Tuesdays, at Village Market, Muthaiga, on Fridays and at the Yaya Centre on Sundays.

Shopping malls

If you are a serious shopaholic, fear not. Nairobi has more shopping malls than anywhere in Africa north of Johannesburg. Goods are more expensive, but the selection is wide, prices are fixed, there is no one to hassle you, and they come with banks, ATMs and clean toilets, as well as with places to eat and have coffee. Most popular are Sarit Centre in Westlands and the Village Market in Muthaiga, which serves the large United Nations population in the city.

Children

Children are warmly welcomed at the Kenya Coast and many hotels have a wide range of programmes and facilities, just for kids. This is especially so in the bigger resorts, where there may also be staff specially allocated to children's activities. There will also likely be both indoor as well as outdoor play areas. A few of the big resorts will have areas set aside as 'quiet zones', where no children are allowed, together, of course, with 'noisy zones', where kids can play with impunity.

Most of the normal water-related beach activities appeal to kids. These include snorkelling, kayaking, banana-boats, wind- and kite-surfing, beach volleyball and so on. Obviously there will be age limits on some things, for example jet-skiing, so do check first to avoid disappointment.

In some areas, especially Mombasa North, there are many activities just beyond the hotel boundaries that will appeal to children. These include Wild Waters, a massive collection of slides and pools, Mamba Village, a sort of crocodile zoo, Haller Park – home to a wildlife park – and go-karting at Mombasa Go-Kart.

Attitudes in restaurants vary. In general it is expected that small children in particular will not accompany their parents to dinner, but will eat earlier. Most resorts have good babysitting and child-minding services. For many, and for couples in particular, this is their holiday of a lifetime, their touch of paradise, during which they dream of dining by moonlight on a tropical beach – so families will probably feel more relaxed in restaurants that are orientated to their needs.

While not a totally rigid rule, in general safaris are not suitable for small children. The main problem is that days are often long, hot and dusty, and the excitement of the first pride of lions can soon turn into demands of 'When will we get there?' and 'I'm bored.' If you are sharing your 4 x 4 with a small group of strangers for quite a long day, young, tired children can be very wearing. If you are in your own exclusive group, it may be more appropriate to take the risk, but in general it is wise to consider whether young children might better appreciate the animals in a more controlled setting.

❶ Never, ever underestimate the dangers of sunburn and dehydration. Children tend to be out under the intense tropical sun for much longer than adults, and it is essential not only that they are well daubed with high-factor sun-block, but that they wear long-sleeved shirts and a hat. Particularly effective are the foreign-legion type with a flap of material that protects the back of the neck. Ensure they drink lots of water regularly throughout the day. If you do go on safari, remember that at altitude the sun is even more intense. This advice applies to grown-ups too, of course.

◒ Stick your neck out: get close to giraffes at Haller Park

Sports & activities

WATERSPORTS & SPAS

By its very nature, a holiday in Kenya is based on activities, whether on the beach or in the bush. Beach holidays centre round water-based sports and activities. Snorkelling and diving are favourites, but on the Kenya Coast, anything you can do in water is available: jet-skis, banana-boats, windsurfing, para-surfing, kite-surfing, sailing, kayaking and, of course, swimming. Mombasa also has a range of specialist leisure centres providing such things as water slides and go-karting.

Some of the bigger hotels also now have spas, where you can access a whole range of massage and alternative treatments.

MARINE & LAND SAFARIS

The coast is great for nature watching. At Kiunga Marine National Reserve in the north there are five species of turtles, the rare dungu, and one of the world's biggest colonies of roseate terns. Watching whale sharks and humpback whales is possible and, in Kisite Marine Park, dolphin-watching is one of the most popular activities. The Indian Ocean coast is also home to one of the world's great coral gardens.

Some of the most reputable companies are:

Buccaneer Diving ☎ 0728 999225 ⓦ www.buccaneerdiving.com
Charlie Claw's ☎ 040 3202331 ⓦ www.wasiniislandkenya.com
Diving the Crab ☎ 040 3202003 ⓦ www.divingthecrab.com
Pilli Pipa Dhow Safaris ☎ 040 3202401 ⓦ www.pillipipa.com

Kenya claims to be the world's number one safari destination and there is an enormous range of possible destinations and types of safari from which to choose. Not only does this include seeing the 'big five' – lion, leopard, rhino, elephant and buffalo, together with associated plains game – but also the northern end of the Great Migration, the world's biggest annual movement of large mammals, when 1¼ million wildebeest pour into the Masai Mara from the Serengeti. This occurs annually in Kenya during the period July to November. You can book a safari through your normal travel operator, though for a bespoke

safari you need to contact one of a few specialist operators
(see page 69).

Kenya is also one of the world's best bird-watching destinations,
offering spectacular locations such as the Mara River, or Amboseli after
the rains, which have recorded over 500 species. Even when the lions
have gone to ground there are always hundreds of birds to be seen.

MOUNTAIN CLIMBING

An increasing number of visitors combine their beach holiday with the
ultimate East African activity, climbing either Mount Kenya or
Kilimanjaro. Both are possible for reasonably fit non-climbers, but
anyone considering such a climb should ensure very serious planning
and training goes into it beforehand, as it can be extremely hazardous
and occasionally life-threatening to ignore the need for adequate
acclimatisation. For best information, contact Mountain Club of Kenya.
 📞 00254 20 501747 🌐 www.mountkenya.org

🔺 *The end of a great day's diving*

Festivals & events

Events in the Muslim calendar	2008	2009
Start of Ramadan	2 Sept	22 Aug
Id ul Fitr	2 Oct	21 Sept
Id al-Kabir	8 Dec	28 Nov
Muslim New Year	10 Jan	20 Dec
Ashoura	20 Jan	30 Dec
Maulidi	20 Mar	9 Mar

The Muslim year has only 354 days, so festival dates recede against the Western calendar by about 11 days each year.

Most festivals will not much affect your holiday, except for the daytime fasting month of Ramadan, when many places will close during daylight hours, but will become a riot of activity and feasting during the night. During Ramadan everything more or less comes to a halt at sunset to allow observers to break their fast and eat.

Maulidi is the celebration of Mohammed's birthday, and is especially observed at Lamu, but will not have much of an impact elsewhere.

🔺 *The extraordinary Lamu donkey race*

Western-based festivals and public holidays

1 Jan	New Year's Day
Mar/Apr	Good Friday
Mar/Apr	Easter Monday
1 May	Labour Day
1 June	Madaraka Day (celebrates the first granting of self-government in 1960)
Id ul Fitr	Start of Ramadan (see Muslim calendar)
10 Oct	Moi Day (this may disappear)
10 Oct	Kenyatta Day
12 Dec	Independence Day
25 Dec	Christmas Day
26 Dec	Boxing Day

Lamu Cultural Festival

Held during the second week of November for three days, this is a celebration of Swahili heritage and an attempt to stimulate cultural tourism.

Lamu is a World Heritage Site and the town dates from at least the 13th century, so there is much to celebrate. Although the programme varies year by year, one might expect to find:

- Exhibitions of Swahili architecture and design
- Traditional displays related to people's daily lives
- Events related to fishing, dhow building, iron work, palm weaving, embroidery and mat making, traditional dancing and music
- Various sporting activities including a prestigious dhow race, donkey racing and a swimming tournament

---

❯ Sensitive architecture is a mark of modern accommodation

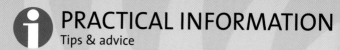

Accommodation

Just about all the accommodation used by foreign tourists on the Kenya Indian Ocean coast is of a good, sometimes superlative standard. The grading system is as follows: **£** good basic standard **££** good international standard **£££** excellent international standard

LAMU

Amu House, Lamu £ Recently restored Swahili house. Very welcoming owners. Simple, airy rooms. ☎ 042 633420

Jannat House, Lamu ££ Built around a leafy courtyard. Swimming pool. Restaurant serving first-rate seafood. ☎ 042 633414

Peponi Hotel £££ Best hotel in 'town'. Nice location. Good food.
☎ 042 6334213 Ⓦ www.peponi-lamu.com

MALINDI

Coral Key ££ Italian-owned hotel with pools, gym, disco and climbing wall. Excellent restaurants. ☎ 042 307178 Ⓦ www.coralkeymalindi.com

Eden Roc ££ A long-established package hotel. Access to the beach but no watersports on site. ☎ 042 204802 Ⓦ www.edenrockenya.com

WATAMU

Blue Bay Village ££ Mainly Italian package holiday hotel. Lovely gardens and a nice pool. ☎ 042 32626 @ bluebay@africaonline.co.ke

Ocean Sports ££ Next to Hemingways. The haunt of the so-called Kenya cowboys, into serious fishing. ☎ 042 32008 Ⓦ www.oceansports.net

Hemingways £££ A first-class hotel with beautiful beach. ☎ 042 32624
Ⓦ www.hemingways.co.ke

MOMBASA NORTH COAST

Mombasa Safari Inn £ One of few hotels nearer the budget end of the market, but modern with bar and restaurant. **☏** 0725 698161

Voyager Beach Resort ££ Good facilities, PADI diving school and other activities. **☏** 041 4751145 **@** info@VoyagerResorts.co.ke

Nyali Beach Hotel £££ The first hotel on the coast, this is still one of the best. **☏** 041 471567 **@** nyalisales@africaonline.co.ke

Serena Beach Hotel and Spa £££ Probably the best hotel on the coast. **☏** 041 5485721 **W** www.serenahotels.com

Tamarind Village £££ Part of the Tamarind restaurant complex. Classy self-catering apartments. **☏** 041 474600 **W** www.tamarind.co.ke

Whitesands Hotel £££ Excellent facilities for a wide range of groups, especially children. **☏** 041 5486534 **W** www.sarovahotels.com

DIANI & TIWI BEACH

Leisure Lodge ££ Golf course and casino as well as all the normal beach and water activities. **☏** 042 3202011 **W** www.leisurelodgeresort.com

Leopard Beach Hotel ££ Nice rooms, lovely grounds, good food. PADI diving and other activities. **☏** 042 3202110 **W** www.leopardbeachhotel.com

Tiwi Beach Resort ££ Very large, with a host of activities. Wheelchair friendly. **☏** 040 320801 **W** www.tiwibeachresort.com

SHIMONI

Shimoni Reef Lodge £ Lovely situation overlooking Wasini Channel, but no beach. **☏** 040 52015 **@** oes@africaonline.co.ke

Preparing to go

GETTING THERE

Almost all travellers to Kenya will fly, the majority by package tour, for which there are many operators. A few tours fly direct to Mombasa but most arrive via Nairobi. It is possible to start your journey from most regional airports in the UK, and then to fly directly from a major hub such as London Heathrow or Schiphol takes about eight hours. It is also possible to fly via Cairo or one of the Gulf states such as Dubai or Abu Dhabi.

The main airlines with scheduled flights to Nairobi are:

British Airways ☎ 0844 493 0787 Ⓦ www.ba.com
Egyptair ☎ 020 7734 2343 Ⓦ www.egyptair.com
Emirates ☎ 0871 700 1777 Ⓦ www.emirates.com
KLM (includes Kenya Airways) ☎ 08705 074074 Ⓦ www.klm.com
Virgin Atlantic ☎ 08705 747 747 Ⓦ www.virgin-atlantic.com

Many people are aware that air travel emits CO_2, which contributes to climate change. You may be interested in the possibility of lessening the environmental impact of your flight through the charity Climate Care, which offsets your CO_2 by funding environmental projects around the world. Visit Ⓦ www.climatecare.org

TOURISM AUTHORITY

The Kenya Tourist Board no longer have walk-in offices in foreign countries, but they do have a good website Ⓦ www.magicalkenya.com. There are scores of other websites on all things Kenyan, with information on both the 'beach' and the 'bush' aspects of potential holidays. In some countries the Kenya Tourist Board have appointed agents.
UK Ⓦ www.kenya@hillsbalfour.com
USA Ⓦ www.infousa@magicalkenya.com

BEFORE YOU LEAVE

Anyone planning to visit Kenya will be aware of the recent inter-tribal troubles in the country. Though naturally this will be of concern to the traveller, the violence was highly localised, confined mainly to Kisumu, Eldoret and the slum areas of Nairobi. No tourists were involved, and none of the main tourist areas – either safari parks or coastal destinations – has been affected by the violence. However, those planning a trip to Kenya should liaise closely with their travel agent about the latest situation and check the Foreign & Commonwealth Office website Ⓦ www.fco.gov.uk for up-to-date advice on travel to the region.

It is generally advised that you have had inoculations against yellow fever, cholera, typhoid and hepatitis A. For visitors to the Kenya Coast it is also most important that you take precautions against malaria seriously. Take advice from your pharmacy or doctor on an appropriate course of anti-malarial treatment before you go. Malarone is presently advised. It may be helpful to take your usual treatments for a tummy upset and for insect bites and stings.

Sunburn may be your most likely medical emergency, so ensure you pack plenty of high-factor sun-block. But also take hats for everyone, especially children.

⬤ For long safari trips, this is the only way to go

Many of the normal off-the-shelf medicines you normally buy are available on the Kenya Coast, especially in Mombasa and Malindi, but will not be easily found if you go on safari. So think about what you might need. Obviously you will also need to take ample supplies of any regularly taken personal prescription medicine.

Have you got adequate travel insurance? Does it include Africa? Would you like to be covered for air evacuation through the Kenya Flying Doctor Service run by the African Medical Research Foundation (AMREF)? See 'Emergencies', page 120.

ENTRY FORMALITIES

Make sure your passport has at least six months before it expires, and that it includes everyone it should. All children, including newborns, need their own passport unless they are included on the passport of the person they are travelling with. For further passport information in the UK, contact: ☎ 0871 050 0011 or 🌐 www.ukpi.org

Check your flight tickets, especially any late changes, and also any transfer times.

If you intend to hire a car, make sure you have a valid driving licence.

More or less all visitors to Kenya require a visa, which currently cost £30 or $50 for a single entry. It is best to apply before you go. This process normally takes about a week and is usually very efficient. Contacts:

UK @ Kenya High Commission, 45 Portland Place, London W1N 4HS
☎ 020 7636 2371 🌐 www.kenyahighcommission.com
USA @ Kenya Embassy, 2249 R St NW, Washington DC 20008
☎ 202 3873 6101 🌐 www.kenyaembassy.com

MONEY

The unit of currency in Kenya is the Kenya Shilling (KSh). It is also possible to use US dollars and pounds sterling in many situations, especially in hotels and at the entrance to national parks. The most convenient way to change money is to use an ATM, and these are common in towns and cities but not in rural areas. Exchange bureaux are common in the towns and normally give a good rate. The poorest rate is in hotels. The main credit cards are widely accepted in hotels, restaurants and shops, since these are commonly frequented by foreign visitors.

CLIMATE

As Kenya straddles the equator, you can expect it always to be hot at low altitudes; temperatures at the coast may be 30°C (86°F) and more, with high humidity. The sun may be severe, especially at altitude, where cloud cover and atmospheric protection is less. So beware of the potential for sunburn and for dehydration.

On safari, with the increase in altitude, temperatures are lower, more like a warm summer day in northern Europe, at 25–27°C (77–80°F); the nights may even feel cold, and the early morning game drive bracing.

Rain normally occurs in Kenya twice a year, with the short rains approximately November–December and the long rains April–May. But it rarely rains all day, and even the rainy season can be very pleasant.

BAGGAGE ALLOWANCE

The normal baggage allowance for international flights is 20 kg (44 lb), though some airlines sometimes do offer more as a marketing ploy. Check before you go. Internal airlines in Kenya normally have an allowance of 15 kg (33 lb), though this is often flexibly interpreted. Again, check before you leave. One consideration is the hold space in the small aircraft you may use if you go on safari. Avoid carrying oversized luggage: it's better to use several smaller bags.

In recent years there has been a new, stricter interpretation of cabin baggage rules. They are often enforced to the letter, with no more than one item of hand luggage per person and a limit of 100 ml (3½ fl oz) for liquids, gels and creams, each to be in a seperate container, in a sealed plastic bag, allowed in the cabin. However, some UK airports have relaxed these slightly at the time of writing; again, it is best to check with your airline and/or airport before you travel. Large items such as surfboards and golf clubs are normally charged extra.

During your stay

AIRPORTS & AIRSTRIPS

Airports will vary greatly, from Moi International at Mombasa to a dirt
strip at Lamu or in the Masai Mara. The airports at Nairobi, Mombasa
and Malindi are all served by good, paved roads. Lamu is unusual in that
your transfer from the airstrip (on the adjacent island of Manda) is
normally by high-speed launch. Safari airstrips will usually be short, dirt
runways served by *murram* (dirt) roads.

Several companies offer internal and safari flights:

Air Kenya 📞 020 605745 🌐 www.airkenya.com
Mombasa Air Safari 📞 041 3433061 🌐 www.mombasaairsafari.com
SafariLink 📞 020 600777 🌐 www.safarilink-kenya.com

Taxis are found at the main airports. Make sure you agree a price
before you go.

In general, unless you are a budget traveller and deliberately seeking
out adventure (and even then ensure you are covered by your insurance),
we do not recommend that you use public transport such as matatus
(see page 30) in Kenya.

Car hire is available at Nairobi, Mombasa and Malindi. Best ask for
recommendations from your hotel. Lamu has no roads, so maybe go for
donkey or dhow hire instead!

COMMUNICATIONS

For a developing country in this continent, Kenya is surprisingly up to
speed with the modern world on communications. Mobile phones work
in most places and the norm is to bring your phone on holiday and to
replace the SIM card for the duration of your stay.

There are a few public phones, normally with enormous queues.
If you do not have a mobile, it's better to phone from your hotel, but
beware of high charges.

Most large hotels have internet access and many have organised a
room or special computer-access area. Some even have wireless access
if you have not managed to leave your laptop at home.

TELEPHONING TO AND FROM ABROAD

The quality of international phone calls to and from Kenya is erratic. Often calls fall into the inaudible 'try again' category; at other times all is OK.

The dialling code for Kenya is 00 254, followed by the number, excluding the first 0. It is possible to use a company such as Simply Ring, which allows reduced price calls. Contact ⓦ www.simplyring.com. This provides normal low-cost calls between the UK and Kenya to both landlines and mobile phones.

From Kenya to the UK, dial 00 44, followed by the number, including the area code, but excluding the first 0. For the USA, dial 00 1 plus area code plus number.

Postal services are extremely unreliable: sometimes they work well and at other times things get lost. It might be worth sending the odd postcard but do not entrust anything important to the system. Post through your hotel reception.

CUSTOMS

Kenya Coast is a Muslim culture. Modesty of dress (see below) is imperative, but important too is remembering other courtesies, such as offering your right hand for payment and not taking pictures of people without permission. It is regarded as polite to remove your shoes before entering some places. Women are generally not allowed into mosques.

In some ways the 'beach' is accepted as a sort of Western enclave, but once you are in the resort, and more especially in the town, the rules of Islam are applicable.

Having said this, in general you will soon discover that the people are extremely friendly.

DRESS CODES

It is against the law in Kenya to be topless or nude on the beach. In addition, remember that it is a Muslim country: it is generally unacceptable for women to move away from the beach wearing a bikini without covering up, say with a *kikoy* or similar garment. In the town, for example in Lamu, shorts are unacceptable wear for women, as are bare shoulders for both men and women.

Some hotels will have dress codes that you need to observe, such as no swimming gear in the restaurants. Similarly, the two golf courses, at Nyali and Diani, both have fairly strict dress codes.

In general it is important to realise that the Western way of life does clash with many things Islamic, so make sure you are sensitive to cultural attitudes.

ELECTRICITY

Voltage is the same as in the UK, 240 V. Kenya uses a 3-pin square plug, so European and US visitors need adaptors. Electronic equipment needs a surge protector. The supply can be erratic, with fairly frequent power cuts. However, most hotels will also have their own generator, so you are not likely to be without power for long.

EMERGENCIES

Kenya has no public ambulance service, but it does have a very effective air evacuation system (AMREF), useful if you have a serious medical condition that requires a modern hospital. Tourist membership for two weeks costs $15. For other details, contact ☎ 00 254 (0)20 699 300 ⓦ www.amref.org. The AMREF office is at Wilson Airport, from which Air Kenya and SafariLink flights leave for the coast.

There are some good hospitals on the Kenya Coast, with the major medical centres being in Nairobi. Private hospitals usually have ambulances. Contacts you might use in an emergency are:

Mombasa
Pandiya Memorial Hospital ☎ 041 231 3577. Has its own private ambulance service.
AMREF (Mombasa) ☎ 041 222 6697

Diani-Tiwi
Diani Beach Hospital ⓣ 040 320 2435. Dr Rekhi is specifically recommended.
Dr Varghese, Diani Sea Resort ⓣ 040 320 2435

Malindi
Galana Hospital ⓣ 042 30575

There is a hospital on Lamu Island but it is recommended you get to Malindi or Mombasa.

For serious conditions it would be necessary to transfer to Nairobi, where there are several excellent hospitals, including:
Aga Khan Hospital, Nairobi ⓣ 020 374 2531
Nairobi Hospital ⓣ 020 284 500/600

> **EMERGENCY NUMBERS**
> **Police**
> If you have an accident you will need to inform the police. However, the police are very inefficient at the best of times, often have no vehicles and cannot be relied on in the way one accepts as normal in the UK or Europe. The emergency number is ⓣ 999, but do not hold your breath.
>
> **High Commission/Embassies**
> **British High Commission, Nairobi** ⓣ 020 2844 000
> **US Embassy, Nairobi** ⓣ 020 363 600 or 0722 204 445

GETTING AROUND
Driving conditions
Driving in Kenya is simply awful and, though driving yourself does offer enormous flexibility, it is worth considering hiring a driver if you have never driven before in Africa. Beware of matatus (minibuses) and buses, which are often driven with dreadful abandonment.

Kenya drives on the left, as the UK does, and there are erratic international road signs. You can drive with a UK driving licence, which you must carry at all times. Speed limit signs do not normally exist, and arrival at a village normally involves collision with an unmarked speed bump, something you soon learn.

Police roadblocks are common, usually set up to extract a bribe out of matatu and lorry drivers. Tourists are normally waved through.

Car hire
Most international companies are present, together with some local ones, and cars can be hired in advance. Do check agreements carefully, especially mileage limits and the amount of accident excess charges. Insist on a careful record of any existing vehicle damage, as even with international companies it is quite likely vehicles will have some minor blemishes. Take advice from your hotel about the best local company.

Public transport
We suggest you avoid public transport.

Taxis
Taxis are OK, especially when they are based at your hotel, and also at the major airports. Do agree the amount before your journey as fares can vary substantially.

HEALTH, SAFETY & CRIME
As a general rule food standards in Kenyan hotels are excellent, but be careful about food on the street and in local cafés. With fruit, vegetables and salads, a useful test is, 'If you have to peel it, eat it. If not, better leave it.' It is quite likely you will have one tummy upset. The best way of treating it is with oral rehydration therapy, or in an emergency with Imodium. Beware of dehydration, especially in small children.

Crime-wise, the Indian Ocean coast is generally regarded as safer than Nairobi, and all places can be OK if you are sensible. Don't flaunt your Western wealth by wearing expensive jewellery or watches.

Don't carry much money or other valuables. If your hotel has a safe, use it. Generally do not walk about at night outside your hotel grounds. Do not walk about at night in Nairobi at all, and generally take taxis during the day. If you are unlucky and you do get mugged, do not resist: just give them everything without a fuss.

MEDIA
Kenya newspapers are not aimed at tourists. If you wish to keep up with the news, most hotel rooms have TV with CNN and also BBC World. Many places also have satellite, and show English Premier League and Champions League matches in the bars. TV and radio are broadcast both in Swahili and in English.

OPENING HOURS
Offices and shops on the Kenya Coast have a variety of opening hours. Shops and markets, especially those catering mainly for the locals, often open in the morning, close for the afternoon, and then open again about 17.00 for an evening shift.

Offices and banks, especially those with air-conditioning, will keep office hours which you will find more 'normal'.

In Nairobi opening hours are usually roughly 09.00–17.00.

RELIGION
The majority of people on the coast are Muslims. There are mosques everywhere and you will see many women fully clothed in black *buibui*.

Inland most people are Christians and you will soon see that building churches is a major growth industry. Often people, for example the Maasai, have a mixture of belief and tradition that manages to accommodate both Christian and pagan beliefs.

TIME DIFFERENCES
The time difference is 2 hours ahead of mainland Europe (1 hour in summer), 3 hours ahead of the UK (2 hours in summer) and 8 hours ahead of eastern USA.

TIPPING

Tipping is a difficult issue. Many hotels will have a 'staff tips box' at reception, and it is easier and fairer to use this rather than try to go around everyone. However, if you have enjoyed special service, it is up to you to reward it. As a rough guide, KSh100 would be a very good tip for the hotel porter, and you might give KSh500 to your favourite waiter after a week of table service. On a successful safari you might each give your driver-guide KSh1,000.

TOILETS

As you might expect, toilet quality and hygiene vary enormously. In hotels and restaurants standards can be superb, not so in public toilets, roadside cafés, petrol stations and the like. On safari you also need to get used to 'going' in the bush, which some find a problem, especially when cover is limited, or the lions are 50 m (164 ft) away. Best to discuss with your driver-guide from the start.

TRAVELLERS WITH DISABILITIES

Provision is variable. In general facilities for the disabled are poor, and there are situations that are especially difficult. These include steps out of large planes when there is no ramp available, getting into and out of all small planes, speed-boat transfers at Lamu, getting into a dhow and 4 x 4 vehicles. Pathways may be poorly surfaced and there may be steps everywhere.

A few hotels at the coast do have good provision, but many, even those claiming to cope well with those with disabilities, have all sorts of obstacles. So really it is necessary to check carefully before you go. There is no specific source of advice in Kenya, but the Association of British Travel Agents gives some helpful advice and addresses on its website ⓦ www.abta.com/disabledtravellers.shtml

A

accommodation 16, 49, 75, 83, 92, 112–13
Amboseli National Park 84–8
Arabuko Sokoke Forest National Park 37

B

balloon trips 71–2
beaches 8, 15–16, 25, 37, 45, 49, 57, 64
biking 27, 57, 60
birds 39, 108
butterflies 39

C

caves 65–6, 92
children 53, 105–6
climbing 108
coral 8, 37, 43
crocodiles 51
customs and etiquette 96, 119–20

D

deserted towns 19, 34, 38–9, 45, 47, 51
dhows 9, 15, 16, 19, 21–2, 45, 54–5, 59, 65
Diani 56–63
disabilities 124
diving 8, 27, 41, 47, 52–3, 59, 61, 65, 69
dolphins 38, 59

E

elephants 60, 76, 84–6, 89, 92
emergencies 120–1

F

festivals 15, 109–10
fishing 8, 16, 27, 37, 40, 65
food and drink 9, 96–100, 105
    see also individual locations
forests 37, 59
Fort Jesus 49–50
forts 17–18, 49–50

G

Galana River 89–90
Gedi Ruins 38–9
golf 50, 59
Great Rift Valley 76

H

Haller Park 51
health and safety 30, 35, 43, 52, 61, 62, 78, 89, 91, 92, 106, 108, 114–16, 120–1, 122–3

J

Jadini Forest 59
Jumba la Mtwapa Ruins 51

K

Karen Blixen Museum 78
Kilifi 45–7
Kilimanjaro 84, 108
Kisite-Mpunguti Marine National Park 59, 65
Kiunga 17
Kiwayu 17
kudus 82

L

Lamu Archipelago 14–24
Lamu Fort 17–18
Lamu Museum 19
Lamu Town 19, 110
language 8, 34, 99–100
Lewa Wildlife Conservation Area 82–3
lions 73, 75, 89
Lugard Falls 89–90

M

Maasi culture 82, 85, 86–8, 101, 102, 104
Malindi 25–35, 97, 103
Malindi Marine National Park 29
Manda Island 19

Mara River 71, 73, 75
Marafa Depression 29
Masai Mara National Reserve 71–5
Matondoni 16
Mida Creek 39
Mnarani Ruins 45, 47
Mombasa 51, 60, 103–4
Mombasa North Coast 48–55, 105, 113
money 116–17
mosques 15, 18, 38, 51
Mount Kenya 108
museums 19, 20, 38, 49, 78, 79
Musiara Swamp 75
Mwazaro 64
Mzima Springs 90

N
Nairobi 76–83, 104
Nairobi National Park 78–9
National Museum (Nairobi) 79
national parks 17, 29, 37, 40, 59, 60, 65, 71–5, 78–9, 84–94

P
Pemba 69
phones and internet 118–19
post 119

R
religion 8, 15, 18, 19, 109, 119–20, 123
rhinos 76, 83, 90
Riyadha Mosque 15, 18

S
sable antelopes 94
safaris 69–70, 89, 91, 105–6, 107–8
Shela 15–16
Sheldrick Falls 94
Shetani Lavas 92
Shimba Hills National Reserve 60, 93–4
Shimoni 64–6, 69

Shimoni Caves 65–6
shopping 27, 101–4
sitatungas 82
snakes 38, 91
snorkelling 8, 21, 43, 53, 62, 65, 69
spas and treatments 107
surfing 30
Swahili culture 8, 16, 19, 20, 27, 29, 34, 38–9, 45, 47, 51, 96, 97, 110
swimming 52

T
Takwa 19
tipping 98, 124
Tiwi 56–7, 59, 60–2
Tsavo East and West National Parks 89–92
Turtle Bay Beach 37

V
Vasco da Gama Pillar 29
volcanoes 84, 92, 108

W
Wasini Island 59, 64, 65, 66
Watamu 36–44
Watamu Marine National Park 29, 40
water park 53
watersports 8, 21, 27, 30, 41, 43, 47, 51–3, 59, 61–2, 65, 69, 105, 107
whales and whale sharks 38, 59
wildebeest 71, 73–4
wildlife migration 71, 73–4, 107
wildlife park 51

Z
zebras 71, 73–4, 82

FIND THE LATEST HOTSPOT

Get more from your holiday and discover the best restaurants, bars, beaches and family-friendly attractions with these handy pocket guides. Our wide range covers over 45 destinations:

Algarve
Bali
Brazil
Bulgaria:
  Black Sea Resorts
Corfu
Corsica
Costa Blanca
Costa Brava &
Costa Dorada
Costa del Sol &
Costa de Almeria
Côte D'Azur
Crete
Croatia
Cuba
Cyprus
Dominican Republic
Egypt:
  Red Sea Resorts
Fuerteventura
Gibraltar
Goa
Gran Canaria
Guernsey
Halkidiki
Hawaii
Ibiza
Ionian Islands

Jamaica
Jersey
Kenya:
  Indian Ocean
  Resorts
Lanzarote
Madeira
Maldives
Mallorca
Malta
Menorca
Mexico
Morocco
Neapolitan Riviera
Orlando
Rhodes & Kos
Santorini
Sardinia
Sicily
Sri Lanka
Tenerife
Thailand
Tunisia
Turkey –
  Aegean Coast
  Lycian Coast
  Mediterranean
  Coast

Available from all good bookshops, your local Thomas Cook travel store or browse and buy on-line at www.thomascookpublishing.com

Thomas Cook
Publishing

ACKNOWLEDGEMENTS

The publishers would like to thank the following individuals and organisations for providing their copyright photographs for this book:

World Pictures/Photoshot (pages 70, 100); Pete Morkel (page 83); all the rest, David Watson

Project editor: Penny Isaac
Layout: Donna Pedley
Proofreader: Kelly Walker
Indexer: Karolin Thomas

Send your thoughts to
books@thomascook.com

- Found a beach bar, peaceful stretch of sand or must-see sight that we don't feature?
- Like to tip us off about any information that needs a little updating?
- Want to tell us what you love about this handy little guidebook and, more importantly, how we can make it even handier?

Then here's your chance to tell all! Send us ideas, discoveries and recommendations today and then look out for your valuable input in the next edition of this title.

Email to the above address or write to:
HotSpots Series Editor, Thomas Cook Publishing, PO Box 227, Unit 9, Coningsby Road, Peterborough PE3 8SB, UK.